DEAR MUFFO

DEAR MUFFO

35 YEARS IN THE FAST LANE

Harold Conrad

Introduction by Budd Schulberg
Foreword by Norman Mailer

STEIN AND DAY/*Publishers*/New York

First published in 1982
Copyright © 1982 by Harold Conrad
All rights reserved
Designed by Louis A. Ditizio
Printed in the United States of America
STEIN AND DAY/*Publishers*
Scarborough House
Briarcliff Manor, N.Y. 10510

Library of Congress Cataloging in Publication Data

Conrad, Harold.
  Dear Muffo.

  Includes index.
  1. Conrad, Harold. 2. Muffo. 3. Journalists—United States—
Correspondence. I. Muffo. II. Title.
PN4874.C655A32   070′.92′4 [B]   81-40811
ISBN 0-8128-2842-9   AACR2

**To
Dora,
Mara,
and
Casey**

Introduction
by BUDD SCHULBERG

Harold Conrad is a throwback to the times and spirit of Damon Runyon, that cheery cynic, the poet of 'Dese and 'Dose, who used hoodlums and hoofers instead of dwarfs and snow whites for his racy tales of the Great White Way. Hal is a very lively ghost of old Forty-second Street who comes on now not only to haunt but to entertain us in a style so marrow-deeply American that we savor it for its breezy impudence.

Our friendship goes back to the days when Joe Louis was a promising contender, when Frankie Carbo was boxing commissioner, without portfolio, and when Hal was covering the Sweet but Impure Science for the *Brooklyn Eagle*. We went to Garden fights together and dug Fifty-second Street jazz in the days when not only Damon Runyon but the characters he limned with such accurate good humor hung out at Lindy's. If you objected to the official curfew on booze at four A.M., there was always Carr's bottle club on Fifth Avenue, a luxurious hangout for thirsty insomniacs where Hal and I would rap about fighters and writers until the respectable ninety-five percent of the city were on their way to their nine-to-fives.

I remember a China doll from the Copa Hal used to squire,

when I was trying to match drinks with Broadway and film star Isabel Jewell; and how we survived a surprise raid on Carr's without getting busted. There was always something existentialist about Hal's adventurous career. Maybe that's what attracts people like Norman Mailer and a lot of other doers and goers to him. Long before the word had new meaning in the Sixties, Hal had a sense of *happenings*. A literary soldier of fortune in a world of guys and dolls, he was bemused by major wise guys like Lucky Luciano, Meyer Lansky and Joe Adonis. At the same time, he was drawn to and could conversationally hold his own with literary godfathers like Erich Remarque, Ernest Hemingway, Nelson Algren and Ben Hecht, and friends like Jim Bishop, and spirits like James Baldwin.

When he moved on from newspaper and screen writing to fight promoting, Conrad had the wit to flavor his title fights with attendance by the novelists he knew. His Liston-Patterson and Ali-Liston promotions were class acts. He combined literary flair with Broadway theatricality to create fistic soirées that veteran writers look back on with nostalgia. The fight game never had it so good. Neither did the writers.

Years ago, when this writer was working on a fight novel and reaching for a pivotal character on which to turn the tale, Harold Conrad came to mind: hence "Eddie Lewis," who seemed just the right balance of Eighth Avenue cynicism and social conscience. The chemistry worked, and when the book moved onto the screen, it was not too surprising that Humphrey Bogart (alas, in his final film) should be cast as Conrad/Lewis. There was the same ambivalence of tough guy and human sensibility. Recently, we caught *The Harder They Fall* on a late-late. Close your eyes, and the legendary Bogie sounds like our very own Hal Conrad.

Conrad's finest hour may have been his effort on behalf of

Muhammad Ali, when the controversial champion of the Sixties and Seventies was dethroned and driven into fistic exile for his opposition to the Vietnam War. As this writer saw when he set up his Writers Workshop in Watts, Ali's brash slogan "The Viet Cong never called me nigger" became a rallying cry for the young ghetto blacks resisting the draft. Conrad was neither an advocate of black power nor exactly a civil-rights activist, but he had been instrumental in getting young Cassius the title shot against Liston and had become one of Clay/Ali's closest honky friends. He also knew there would be no serious money for the heavyweight title until the usurper, Joe Frazier, proved his right to that title in a shoot-out with Ali.

We watched Conrad as he roamed the continent year after year in search of a ring for "The Fight of the Century." He tried Canada, Baja California and states beyond the jurisdiction of the self-important bureaucrats who ran the commissions. Every time he thought he had it made, someone threw a patriotic monkey wrench into Conrad's wheel. At last he helped jawbone a fight in Georgia, of all places, against perennial white hope Jerry Quarry, something neither the Honorable Elijah Muhammad, Sidney Poitier, Bill Cosby nor the Reverend Jesse Jackson had been able to do. Thanks to Conrad, who even helped set up the ring and personally arrange the chairs that wild night in Atlanta, Ali was on the road back to national acceptance as world champion.

Tall, lean and dapper, a cross between *Guys and Dolls'* Sky Masterson and Jacques Tati's Monsieur Hulot, complete with slender black umbrella, Conrad got around. The photographs on the walls in the large apartment he and his extraordinary wife, Mara, have kept for the past twenty-two years on the Upper West Side of Manhattan tell the story: Conrad with Earl Wilson at a splashy press dinner, Conrad crossing from France on the *Queen Mary*, Conrad with a matador's cape in Spain, Conrad landing in Cuba, Conrad with General George Marshall, Conrad with Oscar Levant, Conrad with the Beatles, Conrad with Patterson and Liston, Joe Louis and Max Schmeling, Conrad with Marianne Moore and Muhammad Ali at Toots Shor's. Oh he got around: as much at home in the backrooms of the fight world as in literary circles. He wrote *The Battle of Apache Pass*, which sold a million copies (at twenty-five cents in the Fifties), ghosted a novel (for a well-known comic) that he admits is a haircut on *Sammy*, and he's got a screen credit on *Sunny Side of the Street*. He was also the only one I ever saw stand up to the baleful Sonny Liston.

If Hal brought new colors to the palette of pugilistica, even more exotic hues were added by his lifelong mate, the one-of-a-kind musical comedy scene-stealer, Mara Lynn. A long-legged dancer who could sing, and camp and time her laughs like all the great comics with whom she worked—from Groucho and Harpo to Berle and Hope—Mara was marvelously malevolent in Norman Mailer's play *Deer Park*. Whether she was touring with Steve "Sammy" Lawrence in *Pal Joey*, or bringing her inimitable presence to the movie *Let's Make Love* (starring another inimitable, Marilyn Monroe), Mara Lynn Conrad was a one-girl riot.

But looking back over the years I've known Hal and Mara—presiding over championship fights and unique parties of novelists, prize fighters, sports writers, Broadway biggies, models and wandering poets—I'd say Mara's greatest role is playing *Mara*. In Hollywood and in the theater I've known ladies who worked at being zanies, under the illusion that they were madcap Zelda Fitzgeralds incarnate. Mara doesn't have to work at it. As a free spirit with a creative zest for life that suggests sweet madness, Mara brought to Hal's fight world an unpredictable theatricality that leaves a yawning void when she doesn't make the scene.

Whenever I covered a title fight, the first person I would touch base with would be Mara, because managers could make boastful predictions and trainers could run down the stats on weight, condition, and rounds of sparring, but only Mara was involved in the emotions of the fighters and the mounting drama of Fight Week. It was from Mara that I gleaned some of Sonny Liston's interior mysteries as he prepared first for awed Floyd Patterson, then for self-propelled Muhammad Ali.

As Hollywood stars dress up for major film premieres, Mara would dress for the major fight Hal was staging. The congenial company of boxing writers Hal always courted liked to speculate at the press bar as to what new wonder of fashion Mara would contribute to The Night of The Fight. There was the evening she appeared in sequins with provocative split skirt and plunging neckline, trailing boa feathers, circling the inner ringside with all the flounce and bounce she had lavished on *No No Nanette* and *New Girl in Town*. On her third time around, a gravel-voice called out, "Okay lady, we seen the dress. Now le'see the fight." There was a night in Florida with Mara in ermine coat over slinky satin pajamas, topped by an authentic aviator's helmet, vintage 1940. Which prompted this writer to muse some years later, "You know, I don't remember what fight that was—but I remember the costume."

I also remember Hal and Mara's happening in Dublin, where Ali fought the fifth-ranked Al "Blue" Lewis. It was Dublin's biggest fight outside of a pub in years. In 1923 Battling Siki had had the temerity to defend his light-heavyweight title there against Mike McTigue on St. Patrick's Day. (Needless to say who won.) Giving Hal that fight to promote was Ali's way of paying him off in part for the years Hal had devoted to getting Ali a pay-night, even a shot at the title that had been stripped from him for refusing to bear arms in Vietnam. I flew to Dublin not so much to see a fight as to see Hal and Mara in action—and did they ever do it up green! In a lavish suite in the venerable Gresham Hotel, the Conrads held court over that deliciously mixed company they knew how to attract. There was the old gallant, John Huston, up from his horsey estate in Galway. Stars from the Abbey Theater across the street filled the room with beautiful talk. Gun-runners for the IRA were, Hal found out later, literally making deals in the bedroom. Peter O'Toole was there, and three choir-boy killers for the Provisionals, incredibly casual about a night of terror they had survived in Belfast just two days earlier. There were two former light-heavyweight champions, José Torres, now writing for the *Village Voice,* and Billy Conn, a cynical Irishman from Pittsburgh who had extended Joe Louis in his prime, and who was now complaining loudly of the dullness of his ancestors' motherland. And Ulick O'Connor, the biographer of Brendan Behan, who took me to see Brendan's mother in a nursing home. "She's playin' hookey," said the Sister/nurse. "Ay, then I know where to find her," said Ulick, and indeed he did, at a cosy pub two blocks from the Home, where she was enjoying the happy hour with two toothless biddies who invited us to join them for Irish neat washed down with Harp.

In that mad-hatter week, the Conrads had a neighbor down the corridor, another Irish American, Ronnie Reagan, with his son Ron. Now Ronnie was saying he was proud to know the great Ali, though as governor he had banned him from fighting in California, waving the flag against the draft-dodger. For excitement I drove Mara out to Ali's headquarters in the green countryside outside of Dublin. On the way back, reverting to American ways, I drove all the way on the wrong side of the road, side-swiping almost every car I passed. Driving to the fight with Pete Hamill was vehicular misadventure again, with honking cars coming at me head-on, while I sliced the sides of others parked on what seemed to me the wrong side of the street.

No, the fight scene as produced by Hal and Mara Conrad was never meant to be uneventful. One New Year's we wound up at dawn at a favorite haunt, P. J. Clarke's. In swaggered the Raging Bull himself, old middleweight champ Jake LaMotta. As a rule, I have found prizefighters outside the ring to be peace-loving citizens, courteous, congenial and often lovable: under- rather than overbearing. Every rule has its exception: Jake LaMotta is exceptionally unlovable. The movie did him justice, you might say. Although the ending, lifting my lines from *On the Waterfront*, may sentimentalize him. Jake's way of endearing himself to you is to sit down with you and your girl, grab her as if it were a joke, and then kiss her on the mouth, French style, only Jake isn't French. Call it oral rape. The escort or mate usually looks away, embarrassed, remembering the Bull's great stands against Sugar Ray Robinson, and not wanting to make a scene.

That's what Hal and I were doing, looking at each other and wondering how to deal with this Neanderthal who was starting to make his move. Meanwhile, Mara was taking things into her own hands. She knew better than to throw one shot at a counter-puncher like LaMotta who was famous for never going down, not once in all five fights with Robinson.

Mara blithely poured the full contents of her rum and coke over the top of his head. All of Sugar Ray's punches strung together didn't hurt as much. He sat in abject humiliation, the ice cubes, garnished with a slice of lime, nestled in his curly hair as the booze streamed down his face. The vincible Jake skulked off sputtering his four-letter repertoire as the customers applauded the rout of the bistro tyrant. We ordered a drink for the invincible Mara Lynn and laughed the new year in.

It's hard to believe that inside this wacky extrovert lives a sensitive poet. Just as Hal Conrad, who sometimes sounds like Damon Runyon and Mark Hellinger happily returned, is a painter of delicate touch.

Conrad has written about his crapshoot of a life in letters to "Muffo," a sampling of which follows. "Muffo" is better known as Bob Musel, the newspaperman's newspaperman who, as senior European correspondent for UPI, covered the Israeli wars by taxicab, enjoyed unique entrée to Winston Churchill and George Bernard Shaw, and was one of the first Western reporters to get booted out of Russia. Musel's way with words gave us "Elvis the Pelvis" and, for Crosby, "Der Bingle." Conrad's way with words in the sixty or so "Muffo" letters that he has prepared for this book gives us a taste of what it was like to move in a world in which Lucky Luciano was lonely in Naples and Hemingway turned down coffee with Castro in Havana after the revolution. The gangsters are there, and so are the writers and actors and fighters. And through it all, Conrad gives us an underlying philosophy that might have been drawn from a Broadway show tune bubbling up from the depths of the Depression: "Life is just a bowl of cherries . . ."

These cherries go down easy. Hal Conrad may have removed the pits, but he knows they're there.

Contents

A Foreword by
Norman Mailer

Harold Conrad says he once saved my life by grabbing a television set just as it was ready to fall on my head during a fight. That is about as true as any of Harold's stories, which is to say, more true than you would expect. I was on the floor (temporarily decked) and the set was tottering when Harold grabbed it. So I accept his account. It has the generosity that attaches to insane events. The charm of these stories is Harold's saturnine, mildly cynical calm in the eye of the vortex of the prodigious and short-lived hurricanes he writes about. If dinosaurs ever came wandering out of the jungle, we would not only have to find a zoo, but somebody to feed them. Harold would do it. He feeds dinosaurs. If you do not know the necessity for this, you will never, for instance, understand the pain he feels when Humphrey Bogart rejects him, or the great love he bears for Erich Maria Remarque who welcomes him, nor his disdain for the Duke of Windsor and his affection for Sonny Liston.

Of course, in this book, celebrities are pushed out of the way by legends until Conrad could stand accused of being a name-dropper, if it were not that name-droppers have so little to tell us—they drop names like coins. The best you can hope for in such memoirs is that the name gives a good ring when it hits the counter. Harold Conrad, however, made his working life out of providing special services to a galaxy of stars in various professions, and since he was a trouble-shooter, a fixer (not of fights but of ruptured situations), an anticipator (of maniacal oncoming troubles), and because he also, as Budd Schulberg says, loved the action, and chose therefore to be around in his spare time as well, he ended up knowing more than just the value of the names of the people he worked for. Some of them he even knew by the way they threw their clothing on the floor. He was there not only when they were up, but he knows how they speak when they are down. His book has the tasty charm, therefore, of telling us a few hard unforgettable little things about each of these high-media artists, and legendary hoods. Of course, Conrad also lights them well in the glow of the people who surround them, all those showgirls and hustlers, those savagely hungry reporters and con men and grifters and unnamed Hollywood producers. One could even say *Dear Muffo* serves as a hard-core gossip guidebook to Broadway, Hollywood, and the fight world, but I think it is better and more intimate than that, and finally more useful. It improves our idea of celebrity in the way that a sharp and practical rap on the side of an old radio will take the interference out of the sound. America is passing now through a gluttonous over-engorgement of interest in celebrities, but as always, our tragi-comedy repeats itself: In the right place at the right time, we always have the wrong instruments to use for measure. Our foreign policy has invariably been run by men who couldn't read a page of Marx without falling asleep, and celebrity these days is gauged by *People* magazine. Who but those preppy editors, those ex-*Timers* and ex-*Lifers*, would have less real instinct for the surrealistic world of the celebrity? So the notorious in America come to us out of the rosy smog of *People*'s pages, and it never works. To the degree that the young mind of America is formed by such lives, our vision will blur. How delightful then that my old friend Harold Conrad has brought his crazy laser to the same material, for it breathes under his sharp light.

In fact, these stories inspire me with a desire. I would love to see them on television, and that is a curious remark to make, for how can there be a form more detestable than docudrama? The surest way to end with a permanently skewed view of our history is to have an actor with a mediocre personality pass before us each week playing a great man. History becomes, on the instant, incomprehensible. But these letters to Muffo might provide a small corrective to such sludge. I can see a series built around Harold Conrad and Mara Lynn and their adventures week by week as Howard Hughes tries to date Mara, and Joe Adonis gets Georgie Woods' nose fixed. Next week, Mara is dancing in the show at Monte Carlo, and Harold is buying drinks at the bar for the Duke of Windsor. Enter King Farouk, with his lecherous eye, and Harold is obliged to tell him to get lost. What good Saturday nights this could bring for middle-aged stay-at-homes! We could see Harold fix good relations between Frank Costello and Walter Winchell, or witness young Cassius Clay giving a boxing lesson to Ingemar Johansson. George Plimpton would introduce Marianne Moore to Muhammad Ali, and a poem will be composed on a napkin by the fighter and the lady. Margaux Hemingway will help Harold do publicity for Evel Knievel's jump across Snake Canyon, and we will be there when Virginia Hill tells Senator Tobey why her gangster boyfriends get around to giving her so much money. Yes, we may even turn on the set to see which celebrity is going to get put into focus this week as Harold Conrad travels back on Memory Lane. What a good-smelling astringent it would be! It might even cut through a little of the miasma of our godawful out-of-whack deranging spirit-leaching on-going static-exhaling national gong show. Thank you, Harold. Reading your book has given back some of those long-lost expletives TV took away.

The Nose

Dear Muffo:

I don't know what I get myself into, but I'm working for the biggest gambling joint in the country outside of Reno. It all comes about when I run into George Woods, who is a big-time agent at William Morris and handles some of their most important clients. He also books the talent in most of the major mob joints from coast to coast. George is a guy in his late forties and his most distinguished feature is his honker. It's not quite a Durante, but it's full and beaked and it fits in well with his features.

I'm waiting for a table at Lindy's when Woods spots me and signals me to come over and join him. He introduces me to the guy he's with and it's Joe Adonis. I know all about Joe Adonis. He's a top man in The Syndicate and he owns many things, Brooklyn among others, where he keeps several politicians, judges and cops well fed and well heeled. He's a big fight fan and he knows my name from reading my stuff in the papers.

I hear Woods and him talking about this fabulous nightclub and gambling casino which is opening soon in Hallandale, Florida, about twenty miles north of Miami. Woods

3

says to Adonis, "You know, Joe, we could use a guy like Harold down there. He knows all the newspapermen and most of the people in show business. He'd be good for public relations."

Adonis sizes me up for a few seconds. "It's okay with me, if he's interested," he says.

I tell them it sounds great but I'm not about to quit the paper for some three-month winter job. "Work it out," says Woods. "Take a leave of absence. You'll get five times more a week than you get on the paper, plus all that pussy. There's twenty-four great-looking broads in the show."

I find Adonis an interesting study since I know him by reputation. LaGuardia once threatened to drive him out of New York but never really did. He's impeccably dressed, speaks well, and has that debonair look they give to movie gangsters.

Adonis has to leave and when we're alone I say to Woods, "What the hell are you getting me into? I could get loused up working for those mob guys." "You kidding?" he says. "You any better than Milton Berle, Sophie Tucker, Maurice Chevalier or Carmen Miranda? I got them all booked in for the winter season and you'd be doing your job like anybody else. It's legit."

Actually the whole idea intrigues me. I got a month's vacation coming and it's no trouble getting a leave of absence. The *Eagle* will do anything to save a buck.

So I take the job and a couple of days later I go over to Nola's studio to watch the show rehearsal, and George is right about the girls. There's not a dog in the bunch and many of them are knockouts. I'm sitting with Woods watching the run-through when Adonis comes in with two junior hoods to ogle the dancers. He takes a seat next to George and

I notice he's not even looking at the girls. He just keeps staring at George.

"What the hell are you looking at?" Woods asks.

Adonis keeps staring at him. Finally he says, "Georgie, the nose has got to go."

"Very funny," says Woods.

"This is no joke," says Adonis. "I mean it. The nose has got to go. I don't want you to come down to Florida with all the beautiful people looking like a god-damned owl. I got a Park Avenue surgeon who's a real artist. He did Milton Berle's nose and he did Vic Damone's nose. He's going to carve you a beautiful new schnoz and I'm paying all the expenses." George whines and protests, but Adonis simply becomes more adamant.

Same scene yesterday. I'm watching the rehearsal and Adonis is there with the two hoods. Woods walks in and he looks terrible. He has two black eyes and his nose looks like the snout Lon Chaney wore in *The Hunchback of Notre Dame*.

He's groaning as he takes a seat next to Adonis. "You got no idea the hell I've been through," he says. He reaches into his pocket for his handkerchief and as he starts to put it to his nose, Adonis grabs his hand. "Just hold it right there," he says. "I paid for the nose, I own the nose and you don't touch it unless you ask me for permission."

Joe plays it straight but the two young hoods are rolling on the floor laughing.

This ought to be fun.

Regards,

Harold

5

The Mob, I

Dear Muffo:

The Colonial Inn opens here the other night and it's a smash, but not nearly as exciting as the scenario that's unwinding. What a cast! One thing I learn quickly is don't ask too many questions; it may not be good for the complexion. Looks to me now like the four top partners in the joint are Frank Costello, Meyer Lansky, Joe Adonis and Benny Seigel; in that order.

There are several guys in the supporting cast who seem to have been cut in for a token piece just to keep everybody happy—guys like Dandy Phil Kastel, Costello's partner from New Orleans, the Fischetti brothers from Chicago, Jimmy Blue Eyes, whose eyes are brown, and Eddie McGrath, a power on the New York docks.

Then there are the players. Remember the old Joe E. Lewis line, "All my money is tied up in cash"? That seems to be the problem of a lot of the players here. Many of them are legitimate businessmen who raked off big bucks in black-market and under-the-table deals during the war and it's a lot more fun taking a shot at the tables with that hot dough than paying taxes on it.

Then there are the dowagers and their sun-baked husbands who ride in from Palm Beach on their old money. Also a couple of guys who seem to have unlimited dough. One is a husky Cuban everybody calls "The General." I understand he's Batista's bag man. He must be; he came in here opening night with a suitcase full of money. The other is an Oriental, inscrutable of course, who is whispered to be the head of the Bank of China in the U.S., which got its dough from F.D.R. That's our tax money and every time I see him put a hundred on the hard four, I feel like it's your bet or mine.

It's weird being around mob guys I've been reading about for years. The only place I ever see gangsters are in the movies and that's the only way I can relate to these guys. No matter how rotten-mean those movie tough guys are I find I always have empathy for them. You know, guys like Edward G. Robinson, Bogart, Raft and Cagney, who is always so good to his mother.

George Raft is their idol. They go to all his pictures to see how a gangster acts and they imitate him. Raft isn't playing them. They're playing him. They go to his tailor and his shirtmaker and comb their hair the way he does. Some even use his mannerisms.

Joe E. Lewis tells me a funny story about Raft. Joe is working the Chez Paree in Chicago, which is a mob-owned joint. Raft is coming through Chicago on a personal appearance tour for his new picture which just opens and he stops by the Chez to have a drink with Joe. Three hoods sit down at their table.

"You son-of-a-bitch, how could you do that to us?" one guy says to Raft. "What a rat-fink thing to do," says the second guy.

"What are you guys so hot about?" Raft asks. "What did I do?"

"What did you do?" says the third guy. "You played a god-damned cop in your new picture. How could you do that to us?" It is the first picture Raft don't play a gangster role.

A few days after I check in, Lansky tells me Costello is coming in from New Orleans the next morning. "He's got something on his mind," he says. "Maybe you can help. You wake me up in the morning and we'll go to the airport and pick him up."

The next morning I rap on the Little Guy's door. (That's what they call Lansky.) He lets me in and gets back into bed and starts stretching and yawning. When he starts to get up again, a black automatic slides down from under the pillow. I gulp and tell myself, "This is not a movie, this is not a movie." I must say I am a little shocked because Lansky acts like the guy who runs the neighborhood candy store. He's pleasant, soft-spoken and smiles a lot.

We pick up Costello and drive back to Hallandale. Lansky is at the wheel and Costello is sitting up front with him. I study the No. 1 man of The Syndicate and I swear he reminds me of my father's barber, except for his clothes. He even talks like him. He's wearing those square, padded shoulders and long pointed collars like Raft and even parts his hair like George.

Costello pays no attention to me. He's telling Meyer he's worried about Walter Winchell. Remember, gambling in Florida is against the law, but this joint is running wide open. "That bum has been on my ass for years," Costello is telling Lansky. "He knows I'm in this joint down here and if he starts blowing the whistle, it might mean trouble. Even with all the juice we got in Broward County."

"I don't know what to tell you, Frank," says Lansky. "You got any ideas, Harold?" My wheels are turning.

Costello turns around to me and in his squeaky voice says, "You know Winchell?"

I give him my best Bogart. I say, "Yeah, I know Winchell. I know him good. What's it worth to you to get this thing straightened out?"

"Where'd you get this smart ass?" Costello says to Lansky. "Does he think he can buy Winchell?"

"I don't mean it like that," I say. "About six months ago, right after Damon Runyon dies, Winchell starts a thing called The Damon Runyon Cancer Fund. That's the big thing in his life. He's been getting fifties and hundreds and some five hundred dollar donations. Now if somebody would give him a check for $5,000, I think it would make a big impression on him."

"Hey, yeah, I like that, but wait a minute. That Winchell's a tough bastard. Suppose he just takes the dough and still keeps chewing on my ass?"

"I didn't say I could get him off your ass. You were worried about him blowing the whistle on the club. That's all I'm talking about."

"Okay, okay," Costello says. "Five grand is just a drop in the bucket if we don't have any problems. Besides, I liked that Runyon anyway." He tells Lansky to draw a check from the club for $5,000.

That night I wake up in a cold sweat. What if Winchell takes the five grand and still blows them out of the water? I had to open my big mouth. I have trouble getting back to sleep.

Regards,

Harold

The Mob, II

Dear Muffo:

Get the check for five grand yesterday and drive down to the Roney Plaza in Miami Beach. I call Winchell from the lobby and he says he's at his beach cabana, to come on out. He is sitting in a deck chair basted in oil and he's a symphony in puce with skin and trunks to match.

"What have you got for me?" he asks. "I need hot items for the radio show, gotta be big names."

"I got this for you, Walter," I say, and I hold the check up for him to read because his hands are greasy.

Winchell's blue peepers open wide. "Hey, that's nice, that's very nice," he says.

"It's from the boys at the Colonial Inn," I tell him. "They really loved Runyon."

For about ten minutes I listen to him rave about his personal war against the "Commies and Pinkos" and I'm waiting to lay my hook in. I know that if I can get him coming to the club he's not going to put any heat on.

"Why don't you come out to the Club?" I say. "We got Cugat playing." I know he loves to rhumba. "And we got some of the kids from the Latin Quarter and Copa. Best-looking line I ever see in a night club."

That night Winchell is shooting crap in the casino. He has just danced through three rhumba sets and he's having a ball. The heat's off if there ever was any heat and I'm the mastermind of the week. Costello says, "You done good, kid." To tell you the truth I think I could have swung Winchell without the check because he's got eyes for a certain show girl from Texas who's in the line.

Bugsy Siegel takes a shine to me and tells me about the hotel he's building in Las Vegas. "I might be able to use a guy like you," he says. "In a couple of years that's going to be the gambling capital of the world."

I tell him that I'm a writer and that this isn't my racket and he says, "How'd you like to go to Hollywood and be a movie writer? That's my town and I got a lotta' juice out there. Some of them studio heads are my pals and I can always get a favor from them."

I conjure up a picture of me going to Hollywood with my typewriter and saying, "Bugsy sent me."

Last night Costello says to me, "I got a friend coming in tomorrow and I want that you should keep an eye on him and see that he's taken care of. Big man, name's Joe Kennedy, use' to be ambassador to England."

Of course I know who Joseph Kennedy is and I'm curious. I find out where he is sitting, introduce myself and ask him if there's anything I can do.

"Maybe there is," he says and he invites me to sit down. He's very pleasant and he introduces me to his friends, a guy name Ed Pauly and his wife, from Los Angeles, and a lush named Reynolds from North Carolina who is heir to the tobacco dough.

Kennedy is getting a big kick out of the show, especially

when the girls are on. For some reason he looks to me like a priest on the cheat. He asks me if the girls come out into the club after the show. I tell him yes, but I don't take the hint. I notice that not once does Costello approach him during the whole evening.

All week a steady stream of four-star hoods are coming through here on protocol visits. They come to look the joint over and pay their respects to Costello, who is also known as "the prime minister." Meantime, Lucky Luciano is sitting over in Havana waiting for his friends to get him sprung so he can return to the States.

The story is they've got a very important guy in Washington pleading his case but I don't understand the play. The Syndicate seems to be doing very well without Luciano and if he does come back he's a cinch to take over the No. 1 slot from Costello. I just got the feeling he's never going to make it.

I'm in Meyer's office the other day when a phone call comes in from Charley Lucky. Meyer looks at me and I take a walk. I'm curious what Lansky says to Luciano, but the less I know about their private business, the better.

It is a very interesting experience watching these guys operate from their side of the fence. They're calculating and ruthless when it comes to business, but when the heat is off they're like the fun-loving bunch that hangs out on the neighborhood street corner.

They still think hotfoots are funny and they're all big laughers, but I never let myself forget that most of these guys have notches on their guns if you check back far enough in their careers.

They try hard enough to be gentlemen but it don't always

come off that way. The other night in the bar some guy walks up to Siegel and says, "Hey, you're Bugsy Siegel, aren't you?" Siegel whacks him back and forth across the nose a couple of times and the guy goes down, bleeding. Then Siegel kicks him twice in the ribs with his pointed George Raft elevated shoes. Nobody in the bar makes a move.

"The name is Ben," he says, looking down at the guy and he spells it out, "B-e-n, Ben Siegel, and don't you ever forget it." He straightens his tie, pats his hair down and walks off and I'm waiting for the director to say, "Cut." Raft never played this scene better.

Costello says, "That's very bad manners. He never should'a kicked him."

If you want to put out a contract on anybody, let me know. I can get it for you wholesale.

Regards,

Harold

Bugsy Siegel

HALLANDALE, FLORIDA
MARCH 8, 1947

Dear Muffo:

Would you take five hundred for not insulting Benny Siegel?

This is not a hypothetical question because I am sitting five hundred in front here tonight.

Yesterday I hear rumors that Siegel wins a hundred thousand in the crap game, not at the Colonial Inn. Just across the highway from here is a barnlike structure called The Green Acres. The place is furnished simply in Greek diner decor, serves great steaks and has the hottest crap game in the country. The boys around here call it a sawdust joint and the action is like a street-corner game where the players bet against each other. There are no chips and the house takes its cut from each pot. It has a regular crap-table layout and two ex-bank clerks who can count money fast since there is often more than a hundred thousand cash on the table.

Just before dinner yesterday I get a message that Siegel wants to see me up in his suite. I don't know whether this is good or bad. I go up to the penthouse and he's there alone, sprawled out on a couch before a great picture window that overlooks the Atlantic.

His black, glistening hair is slicked down and he is wearing a black brocaded dressing gown with red lapels, a white towel around his neck and the inevitable cigar in his mouth. He's a good-looking guy in this light. Even the chill has gone out of those cold blue eyes. Is it Benny Siegel or George Raft?

He has his feet propped up on the coffee table and I can see the gold clasps on the garters that hold up his black silk sox. By his heel is a neat stack of notes about six inches high and the top one looks like a hundred. "Peel yourself off five hundred, kid," he says. "We had a big night last night."

I hesitate for a moment and then like a schmuck I say, "Thanks Ben, but I couldn't do that." I think I am trying to impress him as a forthright young fellow who isn't part of this league. Fortunately he repeats the offer and this time it is an order.

"What's a'matter with you, kid?" he says. "People I like were my partners last night because when Ben does good his friends do good. Now peel off five hundred."

I count off five bills and put them in my pocket. "Go have fun or buy yourself something but don't gamble," he says. "And the next time somebody offers you money, don't make a federal case out of it, take it."

Tonight Siegel loses a hundred and ten thousand. Since he gives away twenty-five thousand yesterday he is out a hundred and thirty-five thousand. Now I'm feeling guilty. I figure the least I can do is give him back his five hundred. But something tells me there might be some protocol regarding gangster benevolence so I tell Couzzy, Joe A.'s cousin, what I'm thinking of doing.

Couzzy looks at me like I'm considering a serious breach

in diplomacy. "You nuts or somethin'?" he says. "You wanna insult Benny?"

Regards,

Harold

Romance

Dear Muffo:

I always figured I was a man of all seasons, but this year spring is a four-star semester for me. Romance is in the air. I have been dating a lovely creature named Margie Summers who is captain of the chorus line at the Copacabana.

Margie is twenty-one, blonde, blue-eyed and her tale of the tape is extraordinary. She'll never win a Nobel Prize unless they add a bathing beauty category, but I never did have much time to cope with intellectual dames.

Frankly, Muffo, I have crossed that thin line from seducer to lover, a role I have always found difficult to play with a straight face. But all my alarms went off when Margie mentioned something about "a nice little house in New Jersey."

Margie has been a prize around town ever since she hit the Broadway scene and the wolves have been setting all kinds of traps. Although I think I'm No. 1, some of them are still in there pitching.

A fat Italian named Mario Coccozzo has been singing arias to her. Joe Pasternak just changed Coccozzo's name to Mario Lanza and signed him to a movie contract with M-G-M. He has to take off thirty-five pounds before he reports for his first picture. That ought to keep him busy.

19

There's a kid who lives around the corner from me on 52nd Street who's become an overnight Broadway sensation in *Streetcar Named Desire*. His name is Marlon Brando and he's been taking Margie for rides on his motorcycle. I'm wise to that motorcycle bit. If you're setting up a dame, a five-mile motor bike ride over a cobblestone road works better than three martinis and a dirty book. It's the vibrations. Margie says they're just good friends. M'mmm, I wonder.

Last week when I pick her up after the Copa show her first words are, "Guess what, I had lunch at the Stork Club today with a man who wants to get me an apartment and buy me a car."

This kind of competition shakes me up. I'm lucky I can pay cab fares with the dough *The Mirror* is paying me. The green monster in me rises and I can almost feel the smoke coming out of my ears. "Who is he—what's his name—how'd you meet him?" I blurt.

Margie starts to giggle and I feel the prick of the needle she's giving me. Margie is a giggler and if the Olympics ever have giggle competition she wins the gold medal in a romp.

When she's giggled out she says, "Jack Entratta asked me to do him a favor and have lunch with his friend and I thought I ought to go. He calls him Uncle Frank. His other name never came up."

That's when the bomb went off. I know the only "Uncle Frank" that Entratta would be digging up dates for would be Frank Costello. Here I am coping with Lanza's arias and Brando's motorcycle and now I'm up against the Prime Minister of the underworld. Margie doesn't know Frank Costello from Winston Churchill even though she's dancing in the club he owns.

I tell her who Costello is, throwing in all the bloody details I can think of. I could have been describing a floor-walker at Macy's. She doesn't bat an eye.

"What did you say when he offered the car and the apartment?" I ask.

She shrugs. "I just giggled," she said, giggling.

"But you had to say something at some point," I pressed.

"He wrote his number down and made me promise I'd call him tomorrow. I threw the number away. He's not my type, but the chicken salad supreme was the end. Why don't you ever take me to the Stork Club?" That ended the inquisition.

The other night I reviewed the show at The Hurricane. The featured dancer was a girl named Mara Lynn and she was sensational. She's twenty-one, blonde, blue-eyed and her tale of the tape is extraordinary. I interviewed her after the show and we went out for supper. We went out for supper again last night. Plenty of laughs, but not one giggle all evening.

Muffo, I got a feeling Mara's going to knock Margie right out of the box.

Sincerely,

Harold

21

The Mirror

Dear Muffo:

I'm out of the newspaper business, if you can call working for the *New York Mirror* newspaper business. As you know, I've been doubling as movie critic and covering the Broadway beat with Lee Mortimer, who is entertainment editor, and it could be a very pleasant job if there wasn't so much insanity around here. Most of these Hearst guys are looking under the bed for Communists every night.

Jack Lait is the executive editor and personally edits every page I write. He's right out of *Front Page*, a real hard-nosed, crotchety old guy who smokes Picayune cigarettes. Mortimer is his man and both of them are up to their asses in this Communist bullshit.

Every time I write a review, Mortimer asks, "Any Communists connected with the picture? Check it out." How the hell would you check it out? They didn't care how. A juicy rumor is good enough for them. I never find any Communists.

Couple of weeks ago I review a picture called *The Senator Was Indiscreet*. William Powell is the star of the picture and he plays a drunken senator. It's nothing great, just all right, and I give it a fair review. The next day the both of them jump me. "Jesus Christ, Conrad, don't you know a Communist plot when you see one?"

I say, "What plot?"

"Can't you see what they're doing?" yells Mortimer. "They're boring from within, maligning our Congress. That's clear-cut propaganda portraying a U.S. senator as a drunkard."

I don't think it's any secret that you can find more drunken senators on any given day in Washington than you'll find drunken newspapermen, and that's setting the competition high.

These two guys really believe what they're saying and Lait tells me to get the names of all the people connected with the picture.

If it's not the Communist beef it's something else. About six months ago Mortimer, who's doing Winchell's column while he's on vacation, starts a feud with Sinatra and says some nasty things about him. On a trip to the coast Mortimer runs into Frank at Ciro's one night. He also runs into Sinatra's fist. Frank flattens him on the spot. Mortimer sues and collects $25,000.

A few weeks ago Sinatra was booked into the Capitol Theater on Broadway and people are talking like it's a comeback because he hasn't been doing very much.

Lait calls me in and being the great moralist says, "It wouldn't be fair for Mortimer to review Sinatra. You handle it."

I review the show and I think Frank sounds fine despite a lot of silly rumors that he has lost his pipes. I meet George Evans, Frank's press agent, as I'm leaving the theater and he asks me what I think. I tell him and I write a fair review without going overboard.

That night the bulldog edition is already on the street and I get a call at home from Evans. He's frantic.

"You son of a bitch, how could you write those things after you told me you like the show?"

I say, "George, you got no beef over that review."

"I don't huh, you fink. Just let me read this to you." Then he reads and I can't believe my ears. The lead and last two paragraphs are not mine although my by-line is on the story; and Sinatra is ripped to shreds. Mortimer and Lait did a doctoring job on me.

Things go from worse to insanity on this paper. I get into a row with the managing editor who tries to frame me, but that's another story. There's nowhere for me to go but out.

Somebody up there thinks I do the right thing because the day after the *Mirror* pays me off I get a call to go to London on a two-month job that pays fifteen grand, about ten times more than I get paid by the *Mirror*.

The Olympics are coming up in London this summer and J. Arthur Rank buys the exclusive rights to film them. He will make a documentary using forty-eight cameras and it will be released in America by Eagle-Lion, a Rank subsidiary. I got Bill Stern doing the commentary.

I'm off to London in a few days.

Cheers,

Harold

The Olympics

Dear Muffo:

I'm here squandering my British loot after that Olympic rat race in London. That's the toughest project I ever worked on. If they can ever figure out a way to see the Olympics just sitting in one place, they'll have it made. Otherwise you need eight pairs of legs, eight pairs of eyes, and the stamina of a decathlon champion.

The J. Arthur Rank people must be happy with my contribution. They offer me a bonus and I opt for the Grand Tour—Paris, Rome, and Florence. Not only are they picking up the tab for my expenses, but they book me a first-class cabin on the *Queen Mary* sailing out of Le Havre for New York, September 12.

Run into that reknowned Gallic philosopher Georgie Jessel sitting in the sun at Les Deux Magots this morning. He's got a dame with him from Newburgh, New York, who couldn't be over eighteen. He speaks to the waiter in double-talk with a French accent, and the kid thinks he is speaking fluent French because the waiter keeps answering, "Oui, monsieur," but le garçon is scratching his head when he walks away.

I make the mistake of telling Jessel this is my first trip to Paris, and he immediately appoints himself my guide. Then he schlepps me off to Napoleon's Tomb.

I think Jessel gets off the nut doing funeral orations. Holding his hat over his breast and looking down on the sarcophagus, he does a five-minute requiem on the little guy with the spit curl. It doesn't matter to Georgie that he's 127 years too late for the funeral. I'm afraid they're going to throw a net over him, but the tourists think he is a guide.

In retrospect, I must say the British do a classy job of staging the Olympic Games, especially since they still haven't recovered from the war and everybody is still on rations.

The head of operations for J. Arthur Rank is an older guy named Castleton Knight and he's about as British as they get. He's not too happy about the Games because the British don't come close to winning a gold medal the first four days.

On the fifth day the U.S. wins the 400-meter free-style relay and Britain is second, but the U.S. gets disqualified. Now Britain is first, they finally get a gold medal and the Englishmen go wild, especially Castleton Knight.

The Americans scream about the disqualification for an illegal baton hand-off, and many of the experts think it is a bad call. Frankly, I'm happy to see the British win a gold medal. After all, it's their party. Then it occurs to me that if it is a bad call and they have to reverse the decision and switch the medals around, it's a hell of a story and good for a lot of ink in the States.

I hunt down Castleton Knight and tell him about the harangue. I point out that the whole thing could be cleared up if the judges could see the strip of film showing the hand-off. I can see he doesn't like my notion at all. "See me later, old man," he says. "I'm very busy now." I try to find him later but he's ducked.

The next day I corner him again. "I've got thousands and thousands of feet of film, old man," he says. "I just can't lay my hands on what you want so easily." I don't buy that. I'm sure he knows exactly where the film is of the only gold medal the British win.

I go to Jock Lawrence, Eagle-Lion's head man, and tell him the problem. He says he has no jurisdiction over Castleton Knight, but he has a meeting with Sir Arthur, to meet him at his office at six o'clock.

Rank, a large, imposing-looking man, gets right to the point. I explain that we need the film for the officials and the press to review and that it could be a hell of a good story. He says it will be taken care of the next morning.

The next morning Knight manages to find the film and runs it for the officials. They reverse their decision. Then we run it for the press and it's a big story back in the States. The poor British have to give back the only gold medal they win and I feel like a rat about the whole thing.

The British throw a great party the day the Games end, and I have a drink with a very impressive guy. He's a real triple-threat man, handsome, charming, and blue-blooded. Everybody calls him Lord Looey. He's Lord Louis Mountbatten. How's that for name-dropping?

I see Castleton Knight alone at the bar and he's smashed. I

move in to have a drink with him. He looks me over and says, "Young man, you are an utter cad." Then he turns his back on me. Well, I guess you can't please everybody.

Cheerio,

Harold

Luciano, I

Dear Muffo:

The night before I fly to London to work on the Olympic project for J. Arthur Rank, I have dinner at Lindy's with my friend Georgie Woods. You remember Georgie, "The Nose." I tell him I plan to take my first look at Europe after I finish the London job.

"You going to Italy?" he asks. I tell him I plan to.

"Then you got to do me a favor," he says. "You got to stop off in Naples and say hello to Charley."

"Charley who?" I ask.

"Charley who? Charley Lucky of course Charley Luciano."

I say, "What the hell do I want to say hello to Lucky Luciano for?" and he says, "Because I want you to do me a favor. Charley's always homesick. He hates living in Italy. He don't even like spaghetti and he loves getting a personal word from home. Just tell him hello from me and Frank C. and Joe A. and Jimmy B. and Meyer—you know all them guys. And also say to him Georgie took care of Annie. He'll know."

Now I wonder what the hell I'm getting into. All of a

31

sudden I'm an emissary for The Mob on a mission to Luciano. Who needs that? So I tell him to forget it, that Luciano is a hot potato, making the headlines at least once a month, and that I don't want to get involved.

Wood gets mad and calls me an ingrate. Then I get to thinking. I'm a writer and any writer would give his left nut to get sent into Luciano. Could be a good magazine story. On those terms I agree.

Luciano is staying at the Excelsior Hotel which is the best joint in town. We bombed the shit out of Naples during the war and the Excelsior, which was Command Headquarters for the Nazis, was hit. I can see where it is patched up when I check in. When I get settled I ask a bellboy if Luciano is around the hotel much. He says he is in that drawing room right now and he points to a large anteroom off the lobby.

I walk in and I see a little guy sitting in a big chair and in front of him is a bunch of guys lined up and they all look like they're right out of Central Casting for an Edward G. Robinson movie.

The little guy in the big chair is Charley Lucky. I stand there and watch the action. As each guy walks up to him they whisper in his ear—these guys are great for whispering—and he hands each one something. When the last guy leaves I walk over, introduce myself and give him all the hellos. His face lights up and he beams.

I must say I am looking forward to this meeting with a little awe because when Luciano is in New York he is like a king, with the power of life and death in his palm, and he used it when it was going to do him some good. But now that I'm standing there looking down at him, he could have been a waiter at Patsy's.

He says, "Come on with me, I got to buy you a drink. We go up to my suite." The suite is a lovely layout overlooking the Bay of Naples. He mixes a couple of scotch and sodas and he says, "See all those guys on line down there today, they're deportees just like me, but you couldn't squeeze a quarter out of them if you turned them all upside down. They're all busted, they can't get a job and the local cops keep hassling them so they got to stay on the straight. I know them all and I feel sorry for them. Some of them used to work for me so I got to take care of them."

Now he asks me what the action is in New York, how the night clubs are doing, have the Giants got a chance, what happened to Mel Ott? Then he starts complaining about being accused of dealing in narcotics and he cops a plea. Everytime there was a drug bust they say Luciano is behind the shipment. If they find a goddamn aspirin on a boat coming in they say Luciano is smuggling drugs. "Who needs that shit?" and he goes on and on. I say to myself, "Thou doth protest too much." Who the hell asked him?

He wants to know how long I'm going to be in Naples and I tell him I'm going to Capri tomorrow afternoon. He says, "Tomorrow at noon you and me have lunch right here. I got a connection in Capri. I make a call and they treat you like a king."

The next day I pack my bags, then go up to his suite for lunch. He says he made the call to Capri and a guy named Tomasso is going to pick me up when the boat docks, so leave everything to him. We eat on his terrace overlooking the Bay and the food is excellent.

I say, "Charley, considering your predicament this is pretty good living. A lot of people dream all their life about visiting Italy. You know the old gag, 'See Naples and die.'"

"I'm going to make like I didn't hear that," he says. "I get that same bullshit from everybody. Sure it's great to visit, but you can get on a plane and go home. I'm stuck here. This ain't my home. New York's my home. My friends and broads are there. I want to walk down Broadway." Now he's really giving me the hearts and flowers.

"You know what I'd give right this minute to be sitting behind third base at the Polo Grounds and eating a hot dog?"

Personally I would rather be sitting on a terrace overlooking the Bay of Naples where I am but I sympathize with him. "And you know something?" he says. "I damn near had it made. When I'm in Cuba last year I'm all set to get back into the States when some rat-fink-bastard in Washington crimps the deal. They tell the Cuban government if they don't deport me back to Italy they're going to cut off the supply of medicine to Cuba. Now that ain't very nice, is it?"

I tell him it's about time for me to go. He goes into his bedroom and comes back in a minute. "Here, take this," he says. "It's genuine Florentine silver." I see this beautiful hand-carved silver cigarette case.

"I can't take that," I say.

"Why not?"

"I just can't."

"You take it," he said grimly.

As I'm about to leave he says, "You can do me a big favor. I'm looking to buy old movie films. I want to get in that racket one way or another." Somebody must have tipped him off that TV was going to be a big market for old movies, but I don't tell him that every guy and his uncle is running around New York trying to buy old movies.

"Don't forget," Luciano says, "when you dock at Capri, look for Tomasso. He's got everything under control on the island and if you want to get your pipes cleaned, he can get that straightened out, too. And don't forget to tell Georgie I got to get into that movie racket one way or another."

I'm off for Capri in an hour.

Ciao,

Harold

Monte Carlo, I

Dear Muffo:

You must be wondering what the hell I'm doing here. Let me fill you in. Carl Erbe, who is the bird dog for Ben Marden, calls me the other day and says you're going to Monte Carlo with me. You remember Ben Marden, he owned the Riviera over in Jersey and ran the gambling there. He also had a piece of Batista, or vice versa, in Havana. We're here doing a survey on the gambling complex for Marden, who has a bid in for the lease. The only other bid is from some little Greek named Onassis.

The young prince who owns Monte Carlo is anxious to pump some life into the place and if he doesn't do something fast this whole joint is liable to go down the toilet. He tried to spruce it up but it looks like an old broad with a lot of rouge on to cover the wrinkles.

He introduced craps here this season, which is a drastic innovation, since the big action here for the last seventy-five years was roulette and *chemin de fer*. Some of his croupiers took a crash course studying craps, but they didn't do their homework too good and a couple of American hustlers beat them for a lot of dough the first two nights. I win two hundred.

37

He also booked a line of American girl dancers for the show at the very swanky Sporting Club, which is much more exclusive than the main casino. What makes it perfect is that Mara is booked in as the solo dancer and will be here for a month.

Went to the opening night. It's black tie and by invitation and you wouldn't believe the ringsiders. The Aga Khan had the best table. You know about him, he's the little fat guy from India whose followers weigh him every year and match his weight in gold and all kinds of gems. He gets to keep the swag, although I hear he kicks back some of it. I see this guy eating, Muff, and believe me the way he was going he's gonna have a record take the next time they weigh him. How'd you like to be his agent? He's got a son named Ali Khan who runs around looking to jump on all the broads.

Also at ringside are the Duke and Duchess of Windsor, Daryl Zanuck, King Farouk on the lam from Egypt, Errol Flynn—and I could go on and on.

While I'm waiting to pick up Mara, I mope around the fancy gambling room, watching the action. At the *chemin de fer* table I see the Duchess of Windsor sitting next to Louis Jourdan. What a handsome bum. I take a good look and I swear they're holding hands under the table.

I got some time to kill so I head for the little bar which is just off the main room. There's only one guy in there and who do you think it is? It's Edward, the Duke of Windsor. I sit down next to him and order a drink. The bartender, a tall haughty-looking character, is hovering over him saying your highness this and your highness that. He's drinking brandy.

After a little while I introduce myself to the Duke. He

don't seem too thrilled to meet me but we get to talking and I tell him I used to be a sports writer. Golf is his game and he's telling me how he use to play with the great Bobby Jones and that he once met Babe Ruth. Then he clams up.

I get a good look at him once he takes the brandy snifter out of his kisser and I realize I've been seeing those baggy eyes around as long as I can remember. Endless pictures over the years in the tabloids and inevitable newsreel clips in the movies. It seems like he was always falling off a horse at the steeplechase meet or being piped aboard a battleship, or visiting the colonies like the dutiful son of a benevolent landlord. And of course there was his poignant soap-opera romance that got fantastic ratings.

It is obvious that the Duke wasn't looking for any company or else he could have been out in the casino, mixing with the beautiful people. But he is a solo boozer and solo boozers don't need any company. They meet more interesting people in their alcoholic fantasies.

I must say he did tolerate me and when I ordered a drink he would throw me a line. After I buy the second drink he says, "Met your Gene Tunney several times. Extraordinary chap." Then he clams up. I order the third drink and he says, "Your Jack Dempsey was a formidable fellow, formidable fellow." Ordering a drink was like putting a quarter in the machine. After the third drink, he pulls himself together, slides off the stool a little shaky, says "Thanks old man," and walks off.

The bartender gives me the check and I'm billed for six drinks, three apiece. Now I don't mind buying a drink, but you'd figure the guy would buy back at least once. Friendly like I say to the bartender, "Don't this guy ever buy a drink?"

The bartender stands at attention and says real solemn, "The king never buys."

You know, Muff, for awhile there I clean forget that my reluctant pal, Eddie, was once King of England.

Best,

Harold

Monte Carlo, II

Dear Muffo:

Pulling out of here tomorrow. Got a little Peugeot and Mara and I are gonna drive to Paris. Heard a rumor that Prince Ranier is gonna make a deal with Onassis for the gambling lease which means that our man Marden is out, but the trip sure hasn't been in vain. Had a helluva time.

I keep getting the feeling that I'm up to my ass in kings. Every time I look around I see that guy Farouk. He's still King of Egypt, but I hear not for long. He's only twenty-nine, looks forty and might be the champion playboy of all time. Never saw him without his hat indoors or out. It looks like an inverted sand pail with a tassel on top. He always has a couple of broads in tow in what his aide calls the Royal Party.

He sure ain't too popular around here. It will be a long time before these local people forget the Nazis and he was in heavy collusion with Hitler during the war. When he goes out to eat he sends one of his men in front with the royal silverware and gold plates. That's all he eats off and the locals think he's a pain in the ass. They wish he'd go away.

They ain't too happy back in Egypt with him either. Last

year the Israelis whacked out his army in the '48 border war and the government's just about broke. No wonder, the way he pisses dough away. He goes pretty good at the gambling tables.

Yesterday I'm having lunch on the terrace at the Beach Club with Mara and a couple of kids from the show. Farouk is sitting three tables away with a big son of a gun who figures to be a bodyguard. The king keeps smiling at our table, not at me, at the dames. Then the big guy walks over to our table.

"His Royal Highness say you, you, his table," and he points at Mara and a kid named Gretchen. He can barely speak English.

Speaking very slowly I say, "Give Royal Highness message. Tell him to get lost."

He is baffled. "Who lost?" he says.

I repeat the message. He shrugs, goes back to Farouk's table and we're watching. The King gets the message loud and clear. He looks at our table, glowers, curls his lip and actually bares his teeth at me.

Now you got to admit, Muffo, it ain't often a guy from Brooklyn gets to tell the last of the Pharaohs to get lost.

Keep punching,

Harold

Erich Remarque

Dear Muffo:

Remember when we saw the movie *All Quiet on the Western Front,* then we went back and re-read the novel and agreed it made the best-ten list of the twentieth century, easy? Last night I met Erich Remarque, the guy who wrote it, and I met him at Jimmy Carr's, of all places.

You don't know about Jimmy Carr's. It's a bottle club. You can't buy a drink there, you got to buy a bottle. They stick your name on it and store it for you and you pay a corkage charge per drink. It's in a fabulous old mansion on Fifth Avenue in the sixties and you have to be a member. I'm an honorary member, on the cuff, of course.

Jimmy Carr used to be the man about the house in Polly Adler's famous notch joint on West End Avenue and he serves up the same great food he use to dish out there. When Polly's folded he went off on his own. I think "the boys" backed him.

I get in there about three-thirty A.M., just before the late rush starts, and Jimmy sits down with me. "See that guy over there," he says, nodding toward a table with two men. "Know who he is?" I take a good look and say, "Sure I

43

recognize him. He's Oscar Homolka, hell of a movie actor."

"Not him, the other guy," says Carr. I look again and I see this ascetic, handsome-looking guy, but I can't peg him. "Who is he?" I asked. "That's Erich Remarque, one of the great living novelists," he says.

You can imagine the charge I got. "I got to meet him," I say. "That's easy," says Jimmy, "but they got to be skulled out. Last night when they were sitting there they thought they were in Vienna. Homolka's been here since yesterday, but Remarque hasn't left the place for three days. Drinks all night and stays in bed reading all day. Keeps sending out to Brentano's for new books."

Carr takes me over and Remarque gets to his feet, shaky. Homolka is rigid. Remarque is gracious with a warm hello. His eyes are wild, but he's articulate. He insists I sit down and we talk about the newspaper business and new books.

Now you know I'm not supposed to admit I wrote the novel I ghosted that just came out, but I figure the rules are off when you're talking to a great author like Remarque so I tell him about it.

"I just read it, I just read it," he yells like an excited little boy. "I loved those Broadway characters." Then he stops to think a minute. "Your name is Conrad," he says. "I don't remember the name associated with the book. I would have remembered." Then I tell him I ghosted it. He closes his eyes like he is in pain then he reaches over and puts his hand on mine. "My dear boy, you must never, never do that again," he says. "I did the very same thing when I was twenty-two." His voice begins to crack. "It has haunted me all my life."

Now his eyes well up with tears and he starts weeping,

almost quiet-like. "A writer must get credit for what he creates," he says. "It's his oxygen, his life's blood."

I look at Homolka who seems to be out of it but he must be getting sympathy pains because two big tears are running down his broad, Slavic kisser. For a minute I think I'm getting the business, but now it's obvious that Remarque is sincere. I must have sparked a sensitive period in his life.

He gets over the blues pretty quick, pours a stiff drink all around and raises his glass. "A toast to all the anonymous writers and a curse on all the parasites who use them," he says.

To make a long story short, I didn't get out of the joint until nine A.M. It's a meeting I'll never forget.

Regards,

Harold

Hollywood, I

Dear Muffo:

Just getting settled in our new house here in Nichols Canyon and I want to tell you, Muffo, this is the life. It's like a million miles from Fifty-second Street, so serene, so peaceful. It's still sparsely settled, but the few neighbors are very friendly.

Ava Gardner lives just down the road with her sister and further down are Lena Horne and Lenny Hayton. Below them are Betty Garrett and Larry Parks and next to them is a sexy young actress named Barbara Payton who recently married Franchot Tone. Mara is friendly with Barbara and we have drinks with them once in a while. I like Tone.

Ava's got a little dachshund named Rags which Sinatra gives her and he's always up here playing with Chickie, our Kerry blue. The dachshund's got a tag around his neck which says, "If I'm lost, call Hollywood 3-6893."

Whenever I get the chance I pick up Rags, take him into the house and dial the number. This is known as "finding the dog before he's lost" because I know the little sucker can find his way home on his own.

Ava trots over, has a drink and picks up Rags. I don't

know a better excuse to get Ava to stop by for a drink. And she's gorgeous. Mara's in a picture at Paramount and I'm working on a project at Columbia called *Sunny Side of the Street*. All they do is give me a song title and tell me to write an original story to go with it. It ain't going to be much of a story because they're figuring on ten musical numbers and they're going to cast guys like Billy Daniels and Frankie Laine.

This is the life, Muffo, peace at last.

Regards,

Harold

Hollywood, II

HOLLYWOOD
OCTOBER 8, 1950

Dear Muffo:

It's a beautiful yesterday and I decide to get away from the studio and have lunch in my peaceful Canyon. It's less than a ten-minute drive. When I get to the house I see two guys waiting at the front door. One guy says, "You Harold Conrad?" I tell him, "Yes." He says, "You're under arrest."

I say, "You must be crazy." He says, "I might be crazy but you're still under arrest. You ignored three traffic tickets and here's the warrant for your arrest."

They bundle me into the car and take me down to the Hollywood Police Station. I'm due back at the studio for a story conference that afternoon. Before they stick me in the tank they let me make one phone call and I phone my producer, Jonie Taps. He gets Harry Cohn to make a call to spring me. I don't know about this town, Muffo.

Mara don't think the Canyon is all that peaceful. The coyotes ate our Kerry blue last night.

Regards,

Harold

Hollywood, III

Dear Muffo:

It's a quiet Sunday afternoon and we're getting ready to barbecue. I'm sitting on the terrace smoking some primo Mexican and looking over the mountains when the phone rings. It's Larry Parks. He says hell's breaking loose down at the head of the Canyon. An actor named Tom Neale has just punched the bejesus out of Franchot Tone right on Tone's front lawn.

Neale is a B movie actor who lifts weights in his spare time, which he has a lot of. Parks tells me Neale has broken Tone's nose and fractured his jaw. "He'll never look the same again," says Larry, "and who do you think Barbara's rooting for? She's rooting for Neale."

Just when the coals are right and we're going to put the steaks on, a car pulls up. It's Barbara and Neale and they're both maggoty.

Barbara runs over to Mara and says, "You got to hide Tom up here. The cops will be looking for him." Mara says, "Talk to him," pointing at me.

I don't wait for her to ask me. I say, "You got a lot of god-damned nerve bringing this bum up here. He's probably a fugitive from justice." (That was great Mexican pot.)

"But I love Tom," she says.

"What about your husband?" I ask. "I hear he's badly hurt. Why aren't you with him?"

"Why don't you mind your fucking business," she says, and they both get back in the car and take off.

Well, Muffo, I guess no place is perfect.

Regards,

Harold

Hollywood, IV

Dear Muffo:

The day before yesterday I turn in my eighty-nine-page story treatment and yesterday they tell me, "Thanks very much, you're finished." "But what about the screen play?" I ask.

The producer says, "We didn't hire you for the screen play, we hired you to do the original story. You don't have any screen play credits so we can't take a chance on you to do the screen play."

This is like what came first, the chicken or the egg, and I ask the producer how the hell am I ever going to get a screen play credit if I need a screen play credit to do a screen play.

His answer is, "Don't worry about it. You wrote a good original story and you'll get original story credit."

I pack up my pencils, my dictionary and my thesaurus and head back to the peaceful Canyon. Just as I turn into Nichols, there's an ambulance pulling out and I see some of the neighbors standing around. I pull over to find out what happens and it's a shocker.

Some dame has just cut a guy from ear to ear and who's

the guy? It's Billy Daniels, who's in my picture, which is scheduled to start shooting in less than six weeks.

Billy is a dear friend (and as you know, one of the best club entertainers in the business). I go back with him to the old days of the Chicken Shack on Fifty-second Street when he was singing for fifty bucks a week.

I do a little checking and I find out that the perpetrator, like Jack Webb calls them, is a dame named Ronnie Quillan who is once married to the writer, Joe Quillan. They had a little tiff once and she literally knocked his eye out with a high-heeled shoe.

Ronnie is just like the simple little girl next door. When she's getting her rocks off it's not complete until she slashes her bed partners with a razor blade. Last year she gave it to a singer named Herb Jeffries and he's got a pattern on his cheek that looks like a completed tic-tac-toe game.

Just when Billy Daniels is letting her have a little of his Black Magic she zaps him with a razor under the chin from ear to ear. I check Billy out and they tell me he's going to be all right and that the slash isn't very deep, but it takes fifty-six stitches to sew him up.

Nobody ever presses charges against this wacky broad and she's still walking around. I think I'll get my producer a date with her.

Muffo, I have come to a conclusion. They can stick this town up their ass, including the Canyon.

Regards,

Harold

Dracula in Hollywood

HOLLYWOOD
NOVEMBER 25, 1950

Dear Muffo:

Vikki Raaf brings a guy over to the house a few weeks ago named Ed Levin, a tweedy, bespectacled character who looks like he could be a college professor on the lam from Berkeley until he opens his mouth. Then you know he's a cross between Machiavelli and Jesse James.

He keeps telling me how honored he is to be a Harvard Business School grad. Let's put it this way. If true, it's no honor for Harvard. He's always rattling off the big deals he was involved in, but it seems none of them were ever closed.

At first I don't mind him being a regular dinner guest because I'm a sucker for those wild stories, but it's his long distance calls that bug me. So I bill him for the calls, thirty-six bucks. He writes out a check with a flourish. It bounces.

Like they do with Dracula, I should have driven a stake through his heart then and there before he cast his spell over me, but I didn't. Maybe it's my weakness for the absurd.

He knows Howard Hughes and what impresses me is that when he puts in a call to Hughes, and he's got all his numbers, Hughes calls him back. I'm a witness because Hughes calls him back at my place once. Hughes don't call

55

many people back. Knowing what a cool cookie Howard is, I'm wondering whether he could possibly have fallen under the same spell I have. Why would Howard Hughes waste his time talking to this charlatan?

There is a rumor around that Hughes is putting his RKO studios up for sale, but he won't discuss it with anybody. I get a call from Levin the other afternoon and he's breathless. "I'm buying RKO," he says. "The deal is in the works and I have a meet with Howard in Palm Springs tomorrow."

"What are you going to do, write one of your vulcanized checks?" I ask.

"On the level, this is it," he says. "I got the two jokers with the money sitting right here with me, and I want you to come down to meet them. I told them about you working for the *New York Mirror* and they want to meet you. I'm going to run the studio for them and I'm taking you all the way, baby. Get right down here. We're at the Polo Lounge."

What else am I going to do? I got to go. It's the best offer I get that day. I meet these two guys and they look like ready money. One is a San Francisco lawyer I know by reputation. The other guy is from New York.

The New York guy says to me, "I remember your by-line in the *Mirror*. You must know Walter Winchell." I get this often. I tell him I do, that he's a good friend of mine.

"As you know," he says, "we are going to Palm Springs tomorrow to negotiate with Howard Hughes for the sale of the RKO studios. It is very important to us to get an item in Winchell's column saying exactly that. Could you do this for us?"

I tell him it's no problem, that I will call Winchell at his hotel that night.

All evening Levin keeps telling me how important it is that I get hold of Winchell. "This is it," he keeps saying. I get Winchell four A.M. his time, which is when he starts working. It's a good item, Hughes selling RKO to these guys. He thanks me.

The next morning at ten o'clock, Levin is at my door, still breathless. "I'm in a big hurry, can you spare twenty bucks? I didn't have time to get to the bank." Of course, he had time to drive all the way up the Canyon to put the bite on me. "What's the twenty for?" I ask.

"I got to buy gas," he says. "You know I'm driving those jokers to the Springs to meet Hughes today." I give him the twenty.

And as I watch him barrel down the hill I find myself laughing out loud. I just give a guy twenty bucks so he could go buy RKO for eighteen million. I've bet long shots before, but this is ridiculous.

When they come back from the Springs that night, Levin says it was a very good meeting and everything is moving along smoothly. I get an extra brownie point because Winchell uses the item the next day.

Levin comes up with a three-dollar bottle of champagne to celebrate. "We're in, baby," he says, pouring the drinks. "We got it made."

As you know, Muffo, I'm a professional skeptic and I'm trying to find out what's wrong with this deal, but I can't put my finger on it. Hughes wants to sell RKO. These guys want to buy and knowing Hughes, he had to check out the conglomerate these guys represent before he saw them. Negotiations are moving along, everything looks bright, but I still have the feeling something's wrong.

57

As I'm listening to Levin shooting off his mouth I realize what it is. It's him. Levin is a born loser if I ever saw one. He has the leper's touch. "Just tell me where you see yourself in this deal," he's saying. "You can be a writer, producer, head of the story department. Just name it. Think about it. We're going to have this thing wrapped up in a couple of days."

It's not wrapped up in a couple of days and won't be wrapped up in a hundred years. Right after the meet with Hughes, the two guys check out of their hotel and Levin can't find them. It's a complete brush.

These guys were never interested in buying RKO. They were involved in some other hustle. They wanted to establish the fact that they were dealing with Howard Hughes merely to enhance their credibility.

You would think this would be enough to slow Levin up, but not in the least. In the next breath he's saying, "Fuck those guys. I got a better deal. I can pick up a television station in Dallas and I think I can get the financing. And I got to call about those oil leases in Oklahoma," etc., etc. I'm wondering where I can get some wolfbane.

But there is a moral to this story. It's a concise piece of Broadway philosophy I once got from Damon Runyon who said: "The easiest guy to bullshit is a bullshit artist."

Sincerely,

Harold

Howard Hughes, I

Dear Muffo:

Moved out of the Canyon last month and into a house at the top of Sunset Plaza Drive. It's one of those cantilevered jobs that hangs over a cliff. Great view. Hollywood is spread out way down below in miniature and you can see as far as the ocean. For the first couple of weeks it felt like we were just hanging in the air. I kept looking for the seat-belt sign.

See a lot of Walter Kane who lives just down the hill on Sunset Boulevard. Kane is an agent. He is also one of the few guys in town close to Howard Hughes. He keeps track of the starlets Hughes signs for RKO because Howard can't remember them all. He uses Kane's apartment as a kind of hideaway and does a lot of his business phoning from there, so I run into him quite often. I find him an affable guy with a good sense of humor who seems to go deaf when the conversation doesn't interest him.

Last week Mara and I are having cocktails at Kane's and Walter tells Mara that Hughes is going to make a picture called *Two Tickets to Broadway,* a musical. Walter knows about Mara's Broadway track record and he says he thinks there's a great singing and dancing part she'd be right for. He says he will recommend her to Hughes. Up to now she don't meet Howard.

The next day Kane calls. He says he talks to Howard about Mara and he is interested. She is to go to a studio on Sunset near Western and have some still pictures taken. This is Hughes' private photographer and he photographs every one of those starlets before they get a contract. The pictures are slightly cheesecake, but nothing off-base.

Mara talks to some of her girl friends and they tell her Howard is a tit man—you remember Jane Russell—so she starts improvising. Before she goes to the photographer she sticks an athletic sock in each cup of her brassiere, which bunches up everything and gives her a beautiful cleavage. She wears a low-cut blouse and now she outpoints Russell.

Kane calls me a few days later. He wants to see me right away, not Mara, just me. I figure he's got sad news and doesn't want to hurt her feelings. When I get there he sticks a martini in my hand and says, "Can you leave for New York tomorrow?"

I ask him, "What's in New York?"

"You know Howard owns the Jack Dempsey story," he says. "He's been wanting to make the picture for years, but he's had some problems with the property and now they're straightened out. He thinks you'd be the perfect guy to do the screen treatment since you were a sports writer and know boxing. He wants you to go to New York tomorrow to talk to Dempsey. Jack's already been paid a good piece a few years ago so he'll cooperate."

Now I'm not one of those Hollywood schmucks. I know Jack Kearns, Dempsey's manager, since I'm a kid. One of the reasons they could never make the picture is on account of

Kearns. He is the fly in the bouillabaisse for years and he has been asking for a million dollars for the rights to use his character. Without Kearns the Dempsey story isn't much. He and Jack are on the outs for a long time and it is a bitter feud.

I ask Kane, "What about Kearns?" and he says, "No problem, Howard's got him straightened out." Then he says, "Have another drink. I got to run up The Strip to pick up a couple of contracts. Be back in fifteen minutes."

I'm sitting there alone trying to figure this thing out and I know something smells fishy. I don't see Kearns for a couple of years, but I know he lives in Miami Beach so I get his number from information and call him. He answers the phone.

After we cut up a few old touches I ask him about the picture. He says he hasn't heard anything about it lately, but his price is still a million bucks if they want to use his character in the movie.

When I hang up the phone I don't have to be Sherlock Holmes to figure out the plot. It's simple. Hughes has already seen Mara's photographs and the bum can't wait to get me out of town. It's plain there's no Dempsey movie.

When Kane comes back I don't say anything about Kearns. I ask him what's happening with Mara's deal and he says things look great, that Howard got the still photos, but that it will be a while before a decision is made.

"Can you be ready to leave for New York tomorrow?" Kane asks. I say I can't leave tomorrow but I will call him.

When I tell Mara about the offer to go to New York, right away she smells a rat and she don't even know Kearns.

"If they really want me for the part they'll sign me

whether you go to New York or not," says Mara. "So let's play it by ear."

I call Kane the next day and tell him there's no way I can go to New York for at least a couple of weeks. He don't say anything. A couple of nights later Mara and I go to a party at Herman Hover's. He's the guy who owns Ciro's and it looks like everybody in town is there.

The booze is flowing fast and people are sitting around in groups dropping names and feeding each other gossip— which is like caviar to the characters out here.

After several heavy vodka sodas Mara starts telling the story about the socks in the brassiere and how Hughes tried to get me to go to New York. The story's a big winner. I nudge Mara and whisper, "You just blew the ball game for sure, kid. You can forget the picture deal."

Mara says, through vodka fumes, "Let them drop dead."

A guy name Cubby Broccoli is at the party and he is a friend of Hughes. He runs right back to Howard and tells him about Mara shooting off her mouth.

To make a long story shorter, a new dame in town named Janet Leigh gets the part in *Two Tickets to Broadway*. She wears a size E cup.

Regards,

Harold

Comic Strips, I

Dear Muffo:

The panic is on out here. The big studios dump most of their contract writers and cut down on production and like the fall of the Bourbons who were left with a few dank castles and some worthless titles, Hollywood's long-reigning royalty huddles in bewilderment, not knowing when the guillotine will fall. Madame Lafarge just sits there knitting an endless array of television shows.

While the Bourbons were blown away by political upheaval, the Hollywood bluebloods are being done in by The Tube. The new Klondike here is television and independent TV producers are coming out of the woodwork. Even while TV's taking over, the major studios still look at it like it's an annoying dose of crabs that will dry up sooner or later. Many of the top money stars, producers and directors feel the same way about it, but some of them are beginning to scratch a little bit.

Since I was a bum out here when the picture business was booming, I join the revolution and now I'm a television writer. I do some stuff for the Colgate Comedy Hour, a skit for Red Skelton, some Fireside Theater, and I keep writing pilots for new shows. I think I got more pilots stashed than they got in the whole North Korean Air Force, but at least I'm getting paid for them.

Just did a couple of segments for a horrible new show called "Joe Palooka," based on the comic strip character; and bad as it is, it has some redemption for me because I finally make a decent buck out of Joe Palooka.

A few years ago when I'm back in New York, Ham Fisher, the originator of JOE PALOOKA,* tells me he has formed an independent company to do a radio series on the comic strip. He asks me if I'd be interested in doing the first thirteen shows. I make a deal with him, taking short dough because he's promising me the world if the thing comes off. I go along with it because I know Fisher is loaded and he owns one of the most widely syndicated comic strips in the business.

I turn in the first eight shows and Fisher likes them. He says he is syndicating the show himself and that he's going to need twenty-six segments, to just keep going. I tell him I got to get more dough and he says, "Don't worry, the contract calls for options on thirteen more and you're covered."

The production on the first thirteen shows is amateur night and his efforts at syndicating is worse. The whole thing goes down the drain after the first thirteen and I've already written the second thirteen.

You know how I am with legal documents. The fine print is like Swahili to me and when I ask Fisher for my dough he points out a camouflaged clause in the contract which says I only get paid if they go on the air.

One day I'm reading the comic strip in the *Daily Mirror*

and Palooka is saying, "I promised Knobby I'd meet him at Hal Conrad's by eight." I get calls from friends from all over the country who make smart-ass comments. I also get a call from Fisher who says, "See what a big man I made out of you."

A few weeks later I pick up the Sunday comic page and the PALOOKA strip looks vaguely familiar to me. Fisher would run a different sequence on the Sunday page than the daily and it would be continued from week to week.

I read the sequence the following Sunday and it looks even more familiar. By the third Sunday I realize that Fisher has taken the story line and dialogue from the second batch of thirteen radio shows I write that didn't get on the air and which I haven't been paid for.

Now I'm really pissed off. I go to see Fisher at his St. Moritz Hotel suite and he says, "What are you getting excited about? There's nothing you could have done with those shows. They're dead."

"Not dead enough for you to use in your comic strip, you creep," I say. "You get paid a lot of money for that stuff and they're my words and my ideas. Now I got to get paid."

"I paid you better than money," says Fisher. "Didn't I make you a big man in the comic strip?"

By now I'm getting ready to throw him out the window. He sees I'm getting hostile and he says, "Take it easy, kid. I'll work it out as soon as I get a breakdown from my accountant."

Several weeks go by and nothing happens. One day I run into Al Capp who you met at my apartment one day. Al's an old buddy and he's making a fortune with his "Li'l Abner" comic strip. Capp use to work for Fisher, drawing the strip for him.

Fisher claims the Li'l Abner character belongs to him because Capp came up with it while he was working for him and they got a vicious feud going between them. They really hate each other.

I tell Capp about my experience with Fisher. "That's him all over. He's a pig and Ham's the perfect name for him. You got to sue the son-of-a-bitch."

I tell him there isn't all that much money involved to go up against his battery of lawyers. "I think I'll take it out of his hide."

"Forget that," says Capp. "Just look cross-eyed at the bum and he'll sue you for assault. I got three countersuits going against him right now. We'll throw your case into the hopper and my lawyers will represent you. It won't cost you a dime and it will make my case look good to show what a genuine shit-heel Fisher is."

I figure what have I got to lose. That's several years ago. The case is still pending. See you in the funny papers.

Regards,

Harold

P.S. (to the reader): I wonder about cartoonists. Ham Fisher and Al Capp were two of the most all-time successful interpreters of their demanding art form. They earned fortunes, their stuff was read by millions and millions of people all over the world; and their progeny, Fisher's Joe Palooka and Capp's bizarre family headed by Li'l Abner and Daisy Mae, became household figures in twenty different countries. Ham and Al had it made, but although their thrust was motivated by comedy and jokes, they both died bitter, unhappy, disillusioned men.

Dracula in New York

Dear Muffo:

Dracula is loose in New York. I don't think I mentioned it, but I did see my bloodsucking friend Ed Levin on my last trip here. He was producing a local TV show for Igor Cassini, who's still got clout around this town because of his Cholly Knickerbocker column.

When Levin isn't producing the TV show he's chasing heiresses. His dream is to nail down a dame with a fat bankroll who will finance his mad schemes. The dream comes true, almost, when he meets a kit named Dolly Fritz, sheltered, naive and just turned nineteen. She's the sole heir to a San Francisco fortune which Dunn and Bradstreet pegs at over fifteen million.

Levin must have bitten this kid on the neck right off because she goes for him like he's Errol Flynn, and believe me, he ain't. It's a whirlwind romance with some propulsion from Cassini, who okays his credit with Harry Winston, the jeweler, for a $7,500 engagement ring.

Before a month has passed the wedding date is set. They are to be married very quietly at City Hall. Two days before the big event, Dolly tells him that she had a call from her mother in San Francisco. She's heartbroken because the wedding is in New York and she insists they do it in San Francisco.

Levin knows that if an interested third party gets into the act it could mean trouble and he tries to talk her into staying in New York, but she's adamant. He has been spending money like he already had the fifteen million and his rubber check book is about to snap. He figures once the knot is tied his credit will be good. He writes another piece of rubber to American Airlines for two round trip tickets to San Francisco and off they fly.

They go immediately to Dolly's mansion on Knob Hill and there are two burly characters at the door. Before Levin knows what happens, they hustle Dolly through the door and as it's closing one of the burlies says, "You wait here."

Ten minutes later a guy comes out, hands him the engagement ring and tells him to get lost. "We've been on your ass for some time," he says "and we've got your rap sheet. If you as much as call this young lady on the phone, you're going to be in big trouble."

With all the chutzpah Levin has, he still realizes he's vulnerable and he doesn't want to make any waves so he takes the next plane back to New York. He blew the girl, but he's still got the ring, the ring nobody paid for. So he hocks it for $4,500.

Levin is telling me this story when I first get back to town here last week. He doesn't pay one bill with the ring money. He pisses it all away on a front for another deal he's pursuing.

"They're all closing in on me," he says, "the collection agencies, the hotels, the air lines—and Cassini is really pissed off about the ring. Winston is making him liable. My deadline is next Friday. All this shit is coming together at once, five days from now and if I don't come up with a big chunk of dough, I'm going to have to do a disappearing act."

"Is that your only option?" I ask.

He says, "I got one little ace-in-the-hole. A few weeks ago Serge Rubinstein moves me into a schlock TV production company which has been milked out. And that reminds me, Serge wants to do a book on his life. He's got zillions and he likes you. Be a good touch. Give him a call.

"So like I'm saying, I'm president of this company, a company of skeletons, but I discover they got one thing that could save my ass. I don't know how they swung it and I don't care. But they shot a half-hour show as a pilot, starring Claudette Colbert. I haven't noticed any Claudette Colberts around on television. Got to be worth thirty-five grand low on a quick deal."

"Number one," I say, "the property must belong to the company, not to you, and number two, you have to have the cash by Friday. You don't wrap these kind of deals up so quick."

"Company-schumpany, I'm grabbing it myself and I already got a deal cooking. The guys who did Fireside Theater are interested. They'll be in Thursday morning, but you're right about time being short. I think I'm beginning to lose my nerve. I'm going to need a lot of help in the stretch and you got to stick with me. You got ten percent of the deal."

The Fireside Theater guys come in on Thursday and look at the film. They make an offer of $18,500. Take it or leave it. Levin tries to haggle, but they're firm. He takes it with the stipulation he gets the cash no later than Friday. "That's no problem," they say, "but first you have to get a release from Colbert."

"What the hell are you talking about, a release from Colbert?" Levin asks.

"It's in your own contract," they tell him. "Clause says she made this exclusively for your company and that it can't be sold without her approval. But it shouldn't be a problem. We're a reputable company. She's at the Plaza. Just take it over and have her sign it."

Levin calls Colbert all day and all evening, but he can't reach her. He starts again the next morning and is told she is not taking any calls before eleven. He finally gets through to her after eleven and he tells her who he is and what he wants. She tells him to come to the hotel at one o'clock.

At one he calls her from the Plaza lobby and she tells him she can't see him until one-thirty. The bank closes in an hour-and-a-half. We finally go up to her suite. I stay in the living room and the maid ushers Levin into what looks like a small dining room. I peek in and see Colbert sipping coffee. I take a seat close by so I can hear the action.

Levin starts out telling her how beautiful she is, how great she was in the pilot and that she's his favorite movie star of all time.

Her cold reply is, "Let's get down to business, Mr. Levin. What is it you want me to do?"

"I believe I gave you all the details on the phone," he says. "I have the release here, just a standard form. All I needs is your signature."

"Do you mind if I read it?" she says. There's about three minutes' silence. Then she says, "I can't sign this. It says this can be used for TV and theatrical release. I don't want this playing theaters. I made this for TV. Why, only God knows."

"Not in a million years would this play in a theater, Miss Colbert."

"Then that clause shouldn't be in the contract," she says.

"But it's just a form. Please sign it, Miss Colbert," he says, and he's pleading.

"If you'll excuse me, Mr. Levin," she says, "I must dress and I'm late for an engagement." She comes out and walks by me into one of the bedrooms. Levin is left standing in the dining room, speechless for one of the few times in his life. "Now what are you going to do?" I ask. The bank closes in forty-five minutes.

We rush back to his hotel suite and he whips off his jacket, puts the original contract Colbert has signed on the desk, then places the release paper over it. He turns the desk lamp on its side and keeps adjusting the light until the shadows are just right, then he simply traces her signature. "No sweat," he says with a big grin like he would have preferred doing it this way in the first place.

"You dumb bastard, that's forgery," I tell him.

"So what," he says. "Who's going to know? That thing is never going to play in any theater. And I'd rather stand off a forgery rap than face those wolves with no money today."

He gets the *Fireside Theater* guys on the phone. "Be over with the release in ten minutes," he says. "Is the check certified? Would you call your bank and make sure I have no trouble getting the cash? ... Not really. She balked a little bit at first, but she signed when I showed her the light." He's winking at me after that crack.

"It's two-thirty," I tell him. "We better get going." He says,

"Hold it a minute. You got to see this." He lifts a fancy carton onto the coffee table and starts digging shirts out of the box.

"How about these?" he says. "Sulka's, best you can buy. Got a dozen of them. Wearing one of these even when I'm broke makes me feel like I'm in the money. Don't you love 'em?"

"Cash or check?" I ask.

"Cash, baby, I paid cash for these lovelies."

"You might not live to wear them if we don't get moving," I tell him. We dash over to see the *Fireside Theater* guys and Levin picks up the check. It's past quarter-to-three and the Chase Bank on Fifth Avenue is eight blocks away. With the traffic, it's faster on foot than by cab. Now we're running.

As we get to the bank the guard is just closing the door. Levin sticks in his foot and he's waving the check. "They're waiting for me," he's yelling. "They have instructions." The guy lets us in and Levin gets the cash.

By now I'm a nervous wreck as we're walking back up Fifth Avenue. Levin is as cool as a daiquiri, as though none of this happened. We duck into the King Cole Bar and at a secluded table he counts out forty-eight hundred dollars.

He hands me a stub and the money. "Here," he says, "You get the ring out of hock and take it back to Winston's."

"Not me," I say. "That's your problem."

"I can't go back to Winston's," he says. "They're liable to put the collar on me. But they can't do anything to you. You're just delivering the ring. Please do this for me and I'll make it up to you. The three hundred is for whatever the hock charges are. I'm going to pay the wolves off. See you at the hotel at four-thirty."

I go to the hock shop on Eighth Avenue, pick up the ring

and take it back crosstown to Winston's on Fifth Avenue. Two guys take me to a room with a gadget that looks like a mini Palomar telescope. A guy sticks the ring in at one end and examines it. "Yup," he says. "That's the stone." They give me a receipt and I go back to the hotel.

Levin is playing with his new shirts. He's got them all laid out on the bed on display. "How did it go?" I ask.

"Got everybody paid off but one guy and I got to see him in fifteen minutes." I mix a drink and flop on the sofa. He's putting on his jacket.

"Now that everything is cool, you can give me my eighteen hundred bucks," I say. He draws a chair close to me.

"I don't know how to tell you this," he says, "but my old man is in big trouble with Internal Revenue. I had to wire him eighteen hundred to bail him out."

"But you didn't wire him my eighteen hundred, you wired him your eighteen hundred," I say.

"I didn't have enough left to cover everything," he says. "I got a thousand left and I got to give six-fifty to the guy waiting for me." Now he's in the doorway. "I'll make it up to you. Sit tight. I'll be back in a half-hour and we'll have a big, fancy dinner."

He's out the door before I can start screaming.

When I calm down I start thinking about that lamp trick and the forgery. If I take any of the dough I could be an accomplice. That's all I need. Maybe fate is being kind to me.

I guess what you're wondering is how I let myself get on this merry-go-round in the first place. I wonder too and I think it's because I see more action here in three days than I see in Hollywood in three years.

I know one thing. I'm not going to sit around and wait to

have dinner with this bum. I pick up one of the shirts on the bed. It's size sixteen. I dump them all in the carton and carry it over to Sulka's. I tell an assistant manager there's been some mistake. These shirts are sixteen and my size is fifteen.

"So sorry about the mistake, sir," he says. "It would be a pleasure to change them."

Sincerely,

Harold

Serge Rubinstein, I

Dear Muffo:

Got a half-dozen messages to call Levin, but screw him. I've had it. Wore one of my new shirts to lunch with Serge Rubinstein yesterday. Levin was right about Serge wanting to do an autobiography. Could be a hell of a book if I could write it straight, but I have the feeling he wants to be the hero. It wouldn't be easy cleaning up a guy who's been pegged an international swindler and ex-draft dodger by the press.

We have lunch in the frescoed-ceiling dining room of his Fifth Avenue town house and I must say he knows how to live. On the walls are a Rubens, a Modigliani, a couple of Picassos and some other priceless art. His British butler never leaves his elbow and he's got a harem that would make a desert sheik drool.

He has a long list of enemies and I don't know whether all the things they say about him are true, but I find him a fascinating guy and he's been pleasant and gracious with me. Mara is always saying, "Why do you let those shit-heels get into your life?" And I keep telling her I would rather spend the evening with a shit-heel who is interesting than with some scoutmaster who is a bore.

I once invited Rubinstein to a big party at the house in The Canyon and Ruth Cosgrove, a former captain in the WACs, announced to everybody that she wouldn't stay under the same roof with a draft dodger and left with Collie Young, her bewildered escort. Serge actually wept. He was drunk and didn't bother to hide the tears.

At lunch Rubinstein is telling me he is collecting all his material dating back to his childhood days. He was born in St. Petersburg in 1905 and as a kid lived better than most Jews in Russia. His old man had the best job in town. He was the accountant for Rasputin, the mad monk who was shaking down everybody in the Royal Court. Actually his father was the bag man for Rasputin and not only kept the accounts for all the loot, but knew where it was stashed.

That Rasputin would have made one hell of a heavyweight. He really could take it. A group of patriots slipped him enough poison to kill a bear, but all it gave him was a bad hangover. Then they shot him and he was still alive and kicking. They finally cut a hole in the frozen Volga and dumped him in. That's when Rubinstein senior cut himself in for some of the "take."

He got caught up with and was killed a few years later when the revolution broke out. The mother grabbed the loot and with young Serge, took it on the lam. Using some of the precious baubles, she bribed their way clear across Russia to China and settled in Shanghai.

Young Serge must have inherited some of his old man's traits. He was a mathematical genius at the age of twelve.

He was educated at the English School in Shanghai, and after three years at Oxford University settled in Paris, where he went into banking. Then he started manipulating the stock market and at the age of twenty-four, came close to starting a run on the Bank of France.

After he settled in the States he always seemed to be at the core of some financial finagling. He was no piker. The deals were always in the millions. But the big war did him in for a while.

As you know, he served a year on the draft-dodging rap, but he always claims he was railroaded. At the start of the war he got a tip that a company manufacturing small planes was going to get a contract to make observation planes for the government.

He buys the company, figuring he now has the "essential status" so many guys had who were producing products for the war effort. They were free of the draft. But they draft him anyhow and he fights it in the courts. The judge doesn't see it his way and gives him a year.

How do you like it so far, Muffo? Sounds like a hell of a movie, doesn't it? Of course Levin's name comes up, and Serge says, "You would do yourself a favor by staying away from that mashuguner. He's interesting up to a certain point, then he gets to be trouble. I put him in a company that had no assets at all, just to get him off my back, but the son-of-a-bitch tells me he squeezed eighteen thousand out of it." I'm ashamed to tell him I helped.

"Think about the book," Serge says. "I'm not looking to make any money out of it and I'll go for whatever expense money it takes to get it started. I'm taking a house in Beverly

Hills the end of January for the winter. We can work together."

What have I got to lose, Muffo?

Sincerely,

Harold

Serge Rubinstein, II

Dear Muffo:

My Rubinstein book is dead. I guess you heard. Two days before he is scheduled to move to Beverly Hills for the winter, Serge is doing his usual. He puts his date in the limousine for the chauffeur to drive her home and takes his nightly walk down Fifth Avenue. He's back home before one A.M. At two he's still in the library reading. The butler closes up for the night and goes to bed.

The next morning at eleven the butler is frantically calling the police. His master has been murdered. He just finds his body, trussed and garrotted behind the couch on the library floor.

How do you ghost a book for a ghost?

Sincerely,

Harold

Dracula in Rome

Dear Muffo:

I never did tell Levin to look you up when he got to London and if he says I did, he's a liar. That would be like spreading the virus. At any rate I figured you had enough of a rundown on this momser to brush him fast, but you didn't. So he bit you on the neck too.

Obviously you must have said something to him about your project for a TV spy series in cooperation with Interpol, based on their files. He got word back here that he was going to produce the series.

Now I have to give you the latest rundown I just got from Art Cohn. Dracula is on the loose in Rome. Levin has been running up and down the Via Veneto playing the role of the big film producer and he's got Errol Flynn in tow.

Flynn has just finished a picture in Spain and has been sailing his yacht, *The Zacca*, around the Mediterranean. Shame about Flynn. He doesn't draw many sober breaths any more and the government, his ex-wives and other assorted creditors have him trussed up in legal suits.

Errol is the perfect mark for a jackal like Levin who tells him he has an idea that will make him millions. It's a TV pirate series based on the character Flynn played in *Captain Blood*. He says there is an old pirate ship set at the Goldwyn Studios and they can make a deal for cheap rental.

Through his boozy haze Flynn sees it as a smashing idea and says why bother with the set at Goldwyn's. They can refit *The Zacca* as a pirate ship and shoot the series on location, but first he would like to see something on paper.

Levin figures he's landed a big one and starts chasing around looking for writers. He finds a couple of nice gay kids who are squeezing out some lira writing dubbed dialogue for Italian quickies. The deal is he will give them $3,000 for three scripts with an option to do the series. But as soon as possible he must have three five-page treatments and he will pay three hundred apiece on delivery.

The boys jump at the chance, but on one condition, that they meet Errol first. That's no problem. Then they insist on bringing along Luigi, their friend who is a financier. When Levin hears "financier," he's "in like Flynn."

Luigi, a large, well-muscled Roman, is rough trade and lives in a ménage-à-trois setup with the boys. And he is not actually a financier. He deals in currencies in the black market and it figures he is very impressed with Levin.

Flynn has already finished off his lunch-time bottle of vodka when they sit down and he keeps throwing out wild ideas on how the series should be handled as the two enchanted fagellas take down copious notes.

In five days the boys come up with three treatments. Levin tells them they're the greatest writing team since Hecht and MacArthur and writes one of his bouncers for nine hundred on a defunct bank. Luigi is only too happy to cash this affluent producer's check and pays the boys in lira which they blow immediately on new wardrobes. What the hell, they're going to be writing a TV series for Errol Flynn.

Flynn sobers up for a day or two and doesn't remember anything about a TV pirate series. He takes off on his yacht for Spain. Then Levin is tipped that Interpol is looking for him. They want to ask a few questions about some checks on a defunct bank that are bouncing around London with his autograph on them. He takes off for parts unknown.

You got to admit, this is the switch of the month. Levin is saying he is going to produce a TV series based on Interpol files and Interpol is looking to put the clamp on him for passing phony checks.

So there's your first show, Muffo. Interpol is tracking down the bad guy and he turns out to be the producer.

For Christ's sake, why the hell don't we do a TV series on Levin?

Sincerely,

Harold

Bogart

Dear Muffo:

Did I ever tell you that I used to take Budd Schulberg around to the fight gyms when he was writing his novel, *The Harder They Fall*? While Budd didn't know a lot of the fight characters personally, I think he knows more about the fight racket than I do. At the time he never tells me he is basing the lead character in the novel on me. It is about a sports writer who goes into fight promotion.

It is a fine novel and not long ago Warner Brothers buy the book and announce that Humphrey Bogart is going to play the lead. You can imagine how proud I am. Bogart my favorite actor playing me in the movies.

I'm in a Sunset Strip joint one night last week and I see Bogart sitting at a table in a corner with another guy. I say to myself this is the perfect time to meet him. I can tell him I'm the guy he's going to play in the movie. Maybe he wants a few pointers.

I keep watching him and he's tossing those drinks off pretty good. When the guy he's with gets up from the table I figure now's the time to go over and talk to him. He's got his head down over his glass and I say, "Mr. Bogart, my name is

Harold Conrad." He don't look up. I wait a few seconds and again I say "I'm Harold Conrad." He don't make a move. I say, "Mr. Bogart, I just want to tell you how proud I am that you're playing me in *The Harder They Fall.*"

Now he slowly raises his head and I can see how skulled he is. His eyes are barely open. I repeat my line about how proud I am. "Why don't you go and fuck yourself," he says and drops his head back down over the glass.

You know, Muffo, I was never so crushed in my life. I wanted to crawl out of there on my hands and knees.

A few days later I'm having lunch at Chasen's with Nunnally Johnson. He worked on the *Eagle* before I did, and who's sitting at a table not far from us—Bogart and some people. I tell Johnson who is a friend of Bogart's about what happened the other night. He thinks it is hilarious.

About fifteen minutes later Bogart is walking past our table on his way to the john. Johnson calls him over and introduces us. "Sit down a minute, Bogey," he says, "you got to hear this." Then he says to me, "Tell him the story." So I repeat it. Bogart laughs. "Did I really say that?" He laughs again. "I'm sorry, pal, you caught me on an off-night. I apologize."

If I hadn't got that squared away with Bogart I don't think I ever would have been the same.

See you in the movies,

Harold

Live TV

Dear Muffo:

Just did a live TV show for CBS and it was like being back on Broadway, chorus girls, comics and a big orchestra led by David Rose. You're wondering how I got the job? How else do you get a job out here? I'm a friend of the executive producer.

Cece Barker is the boss of several prime-time shows here at CBS, one of them being *Shower of Stars,* a musical with a book. It rotates every third week with a drama called *Climax.* But there is not a shower of stars out here who want to do television. There's hardly a trickle and that's Barker's problem. He tells me if I can come up with a big name movie star, I can write my own ticket.

One of the best song-and-dance men in Hollywood these days is Dan Dailey, who is under contract to 20th Century-Fox, but he can do outside things. Dan is an ex-chorus boy who loves to hoof. When I tell him we can do a musical at CBS for top money and he can name any play he wants, without batting an eye he says, "I got the perfect vehicle. How about *Burlesque?*"

I have seen *Burlesque* as a straight play and it is a

89

schmaltzy old turkey that must be dated by now. "Why *Burlesque?*" I ask.

"Because the main set is a theater and it's perfect for a musical," says Dan. "I know the book is hokey, but we can overcome that with good numbers like they do in Broadway musicals. That's what television needs."

If Dailey likes it, I like it. "Who can we get for the girl?" I ask.

"Who else? Grable," he says.

"Betty Grable!" I shout, startling a drunk at the bar next to us.

"I'm sure I can get Grable," he tells me. "We work well together in musicals and she likes to dance with me."

This is more than I can bear and ten minutes later I'm on my way to Cece's house, getting a speeding ticket on the way.

Cece is delirious. No network has snared movie stars of this caliber. "I'll put Friedkin and Fine right to work on the book," he says, "They're a solid television writing team. And you start thinking about the supporting parts."

I have time to think about them while Friedkin and Fine are getting something on paper. I come up with some names like Joan Blondell, Jimmy Gleason and (I get a brainstorm) Jack Oakie for the second banana. He was a trademark in those crazy college musicals in the thirties and he really hooked me when he played Mussolini in Chaplin's *The Great Dictator.*

Shower of Stars has an in-house producer named Nat Perrin. Cece names me associate producer, a credit that doesn't thrill me, but the money is so good I could care less. I find out there is a little friction because Perrin is beefing. He says it's not right for an associate producer to get more money than the producer, but that's his problem.

Dailey has trouble finding Grable. He finally tracks her down in Palm Springs. She has just fractured her ankle and there's no way she can be ready for rehearsals. "But I got a great back-up," says Dan, "Marilyn Maxwell, fair hoofer, good actress and a helluva singer. She's in, I've already talked to her. And she doesn't have to get as much money as Grable."

I tell him about my idea for Jack Oakie and he says, "Great, but forget it. Oakie's out there in Tarzana, sitting on his old money. He doesn't want to work. He's been retired for years."

The next day I get Oakie's number, take a shot and call him. His wife answers. "No, you can't talk to him on the phone." I say, "I'm doing a big television show right down his alley and he could give me some advice."

There's a pause. "Okay, he'll see you if you want to come out tomorrow." It seems so easy I figure this guy must be looking for someone to talk to.

I'm out there the first thing next morning and it's a thrill to see that familiar grin. Oakie's hair is almost white, otherwise he hasn't changed all that much, slit eyes buried in that great moon face. Although he stutters he still talks in that same W. C. Fields staccato style. Same school.

Before I can tell him what I'm there for, he's asking me who I am and what my background is. I tell him I was once a sports writer and he starts talking about the old Hollywood Legion fights. Then he takes me over to see his gymnasium.

I see the speed bag and I do my fist-elbow number. He's tickled. I figure I'm doing great. We go to the main house for lunch and I ask him if he's familiar with *Burlesque*. He says he knows it well. "Been made twice into pictures," he tells me.

I finally get around to what I'm doing at CBS with Dailey. "Jack," I say, "you'd be sensational as the second banana. You could make this thing a big hit." The slit eyes close zipper-tight but the rest of the face opens in a great laugh. "You kiddin' me, sonny," he says. "Everybody knows I quit the business. I ain't worked in years."

There's a lump in my stomach. "Then how about a comeback?" I say. "Everybody makes a comeback, Jack Dempsey, Joe Louis."

"Oh, you're cute," he says. Then he takes me to the library which is filled with original scripts, and a large pile of scrap books. For an hour he leads me through his career, showing me still pictures, feature stories and reviews. He's getting nostalgic and I can see he's really missing it all. I figure I'll make one more pass.

"Jack," I say, "do you realize that this whole generation hardly knows who you are? There's nobody around like you. And more people can see you in one night on television than in one of your old pictures in five years."

There is silence as he lights a cigarette and takes a few pokes. "Guess you're right about that, sonny," he says. "It's a whole new audience."

"The part is made to order for you," I tell him. "You can do all your old schtik. They'll love it."

More silence and smoke rings. "Got anything on paper I can read?" he asks. I tell him we will have next week.

"Bring the stuff out to me and we'll talk," he says and he bends down, with his back to me as he replaces the scrap books.

I say, "Could you give me some commitment now?" He doesn't answer. I repeat the question. Still no answer. When he turns around to me I have the feeling he didn't hear a word I said. I repeat the question again and he's looking at me intently as I speak. I half-noticed him doing this before, but paid no attention to it. Now I knew. This guy's deaf or damn near it and he's been reading my lips.

"Don't push me, pal," he says. "This is a big decision for me. We'll talk about it more next time."

When I try to tell Dailey I think Oakie is going deaf, he tells me Oakie has been near-deaf for years, but that he's an expert lip reader and never missed a cue. "And what about Maxwell?" says Dailey. "When she takes her glasses off she can't see two feet in front of her. She needs somebody to lead her around the set until she gets the lay of the land."

Oakie signs on and comes to rehearsal all fired up like a kid on his first job, but there are all kinds of problems and sometimes I wonder whether this thing is ever going to come off. We're using a burlesque runway that projects out from the stage and it's only four-feet wide. Mara has to choreograph a tight number for Maxwell that will keep her in the middle so she won't dance off into the audience.

Somehow everything comes together when it has to. We go "live" to New York and see the kinescope here three hours later. Dailey, Maxwell, Oakie and Blondell couldn't be better. Nice to watch real pros working off each other. Jack Benny comes on as a "surprise" guest and does an old burlesque skit in the finale.

We get mostly good reviews, especially a rave by John Crosby and everybody is happy all around, but those wild moments of the first day's rehearsal still give me a shudder when I recall Oakie grabbing myopic Max's arm and saying,

"Honey, you just tell me what they are saying, and I'll tell you what they are doing."

He was only half kidding, but I think that's the way they run the networks out here.

Regards,

Harold

Confidential Magazine, I

NEW YORK
JUNE 24, 1957

Dear Muffo:

Just getting settled back here in the old hometown after six years on the Coast and the first call I get on my new phone is from Art Cohn who's been my neighbor for years in Cold Water Canyon and is probably my best friend in Hollywood. He's in town and wants me to have lunch with him.

Art, who's got all kinds of big screen credits, has just hooked up with our old pal Mike Todd and Mike is paying him a hundred big ones to do the screenplay on *Don Quixote*, his next epic. Art's quite a character himself. Don't you remember him? MacArthur had him kicked out of the Pacific theater when he was a war correspondent because he talked out of turn.

Over lunch Art says, "I want you to do me a favor. Todd is friends with a guy named Bob Harrison who owns *Confidential Magazine*. He's got a piece on Mike and Harry Cohn, of Columbia Pictures, he wants to run and I want you to write it."

I find this a strange request. "I can't see myself writing for the pussy magazine," I tell him. "And what the hell does

Todd need that lousy rag for now that he's won all those Academy Awards for *Around the World in Eighty Days?*"

"You know how Todd likes that ink," he says. "And the magazine has a circulation of six million. Mike agreed to let Harrison run the piece if he could name the writer because he didn't want one of his hacks to do it. I brought up your name and Mike said fine because he knows your stuff."

"The bum ought to," I tell him. "He took an option on our screen treatment and never paid us the five thousand he owed us. We were going to sue him, but Musel said you'd have to get on line to sue Todd."

"I don't know anything about that," says Cohn. "Maybe I can help you there, but do this for me. It will be a good payday and you won't be using your own by-line."

The next day I go over to the *Confidential Magazine* offices to talk to Harrison. He's a weird-looking bird with eyes like a hooded falcon and they keep darting from left to right so you can't eyeball him. He's giving me a lot of bullshit, like he's glad to have me aboard and what a good writer I am.

I tell him I'm not getting aboard, that I'm just treading water, doing a favor for a friend. I ask him what this Todd story is all about, and he says, "Mike wants to tell you the story himself. You got an appointment with him at his Park Avenue apartment tomorrow at three."

"Why don't you give me a hint?" I say.

"It's a straight story, no sex. We do three or four straight stories every issue. This is a piece about Mike Todd who is becoming one of the biggest men in Hollywood and Harry Cohn who runs Columbia Pictures. What we have here is a story of two motion picture giants trying to fuck each other." Frankly I don't see anything unusual about this.

"You couldn't have picked a better day to come up here," he says. "We're putting the magazine to bed today and I'd like you to take a look at the operation."

I'm very curious about this setup and although I have an appointment I stick around for a while. I don't know whether you've seen *Confidential Magazine* over there, but let me fill you in. It's the devil's diary. Harrison has undressed half of Hollywood on its pages with blow-by-blow descriptions of bedroom encounters—and I do mean blow-by-blow.

No one is sacred, Marilyn Monroe, Lana Turner, Ava Gardner, Walter Pidgeon, Fredric March, and down through the blue book. The stuff reads like out-and-out libel but hardly anyone ever sues. One of the few is Lee Liberace, who collected twenty-five grand.

Of course the studios are frantic and the magazine is discussed only in loathsome terms out there, but strangely enough there's not a copy left on the Hollywood news stands the day after the magazine comes out.

"You can make some money with me," Harrison says. "I got a little deal for you, a package, three stories, straight ones, the Todd piece and two others. I'll pay you three thousand and they're short pieces, under a thousand words."

I say I'm just here to do the Todd story, but while I'm saying it I'm thinking *Collier's* paid half as much for three pieces, and for twice as many words.

"You'll love the other two stories," he says. "You know the Internal Revenue is cracking down on hookers. Got a contact in the IRS. Like you to go down to Washington. He'll tell you anything you want to know. Ought to be some funny stuff, the Internal Revenue chasing after the whores to pay up their taxes. Got the picture?"

"Could be funny," I say.

"You kidding? It's boffo, for Chris'sake. The other piece is about Wallace Beery. He never trusted banks. Wore a money belt. Sometimes he had as much as a million cash on him."

"Now I know why he had that big belly," I say. Big laugh.

"You're beautiful, kid," he says. "You got the drift. You're going to do great with me."

I say, "Hold it a minute, Harrison. I want this on the record. I don't want to write for *Confidential,* I'm doing a favor. If I do the piece, nobody is to know about it and if you drop my name around I'll come back here and blow up this joint."

"No problem," he says. "Lots of big-name writers came through here. You never heard their names, did you?"

"There's one thing I want to know," I say. "How the hell do you get away with printing all that terrible shit without somebody shooting you or at least suing your ass off?"

"Been shot once," he says. "Just a flesh wound. I'm not afraid of that. But no one is going to sue me because all these stories are true, for the most part. These people are public figures and the public has a right to know. We're selling six million copies an issue."

I am about to say, "That's the shame of it," when I suddenly realize what a hypocritical ass I am being since I haven't missed an issue of *Confidential* all year.

"Let me show you something," he says, and he goes to a wall lined with files, opens one with his key, leafs through a drawer and hands me a sheet of paper. "Read that."

It's one paragraph. It reads: "I swear that all the events

described in the above story are true and that I was a participant in these events." It's signed "Johnny" something. The signature is scrawled and I can't make out the last name.

"Who's this guy, Johnny?" I ask.

"You read the Lana Turner story a couple of months ago?" I remembered it. They didn't leave too much to the imagination.

"Johnny does some work for us. Works as a bartender around Hollywood. He's the guy in the Lana Turner story. You see, we get this stuff right from the horse's mouth. Who's gonna sue? I'm no schmuck, kid. Every piece I run is sworn and documented with at least one witness.

"And look at that Barbara Peyton. Everytime she runs out of dough she stops by my Hollywood office and sells us a story about a movie star she balled. And she's cute. She left little hidden clues around in case she has to back it up. Then there's the fading movie stars who need a shot in the arm. Unsolicited they give me the stories. Don't forget, six million copies, baby."

"Are you telling me all these stories are really true?"

"Of course they're all true," he says. "Once we establish the star in the hay and that's documented, we can say anything we want and I think we make them a hell of a lot more interesting than they really are. What's a guy gonna do, sue us and admit he was in the hay with the dame, but claim he didn't do all the other things we dress the story with?"

There's a knock on the door, a guy sticks his head in and says, "Three o'clock, boss, time for the story conference."

"Okay," Harrison says, and six people file in, four men and two women. The women are Harrison's sisters and seem like lovely ladies. "This is the final reading before we close the book," Harrison tells me. "Sam here reads our top stories. We listen and when he's finished we make comments. Now where the hell is Charlie?"

"We just got somebody to fill in for him. He's on his way up," one of the staff says. A few seconds later a huge guy with a blond crew cut, gimlet eyes and a mouth like a torn mail pouch enters the room. He's wearing khaki pants and a green work shirt.

I'm wondering what this slack-jawed moose is doing here. In a whisper I ask one of the staff who the hell he is. "Oh, Charlie is our man-in-the-street critic. He's also the elevator man here in the building. We wouldn't do a final story conference without him. If he likes the story we know we got a winner."

Now Sam starts reading the first story in a voice that sounds like the narrator on the "March of Time."

Would you believe it, Muffo, the story is fifteen years old and you and I know it better than the guy who wrote it. It's the one about the cops raiding the weekly orgy at Dickenson's when Walter Pidgeon supposedly hid out on the window ledge bare-ass.

When Sam is through reading the piece, everybody turns and looks at Charlie, who's got a big grin on his face. "I like it, I like it," he says.

At that point I am late for my appointment and have to leave, but I'm seeing Todd tomorrow.

Sincerely,

Harold

P.S. (*to the reader*): There was a lot more between the lines

100

in that Walter Pidgeon story I heard read than Harrison knew, but I wasn't about to say anything. A staid lawyer in his late forties, gray hair, distinguished-looking, kept an apartment in a town house on Fifty-first Street, just off Park. He would come down from Boston at least twice a month and throw this soirée.

The guy's name was Dick Dickenson and he was an exhibitionist. He just liked to be watched and his female partners were always knockouts. He appreciated an attractive audience who would get into the spirit of things, and a press agent who was a regular habitué helped with the invitations and saw to it that the "right" people were invited.

The event was becoming notorious, with rumors circulating from coast to coast. Hollywood stars, Broadway actors, showgirls, Wall Street brokers, society folks were making it. They say it was the best party in New York, with something for everybody. And it was. I made it once.

The war is on and I'm in the Air Force, but I vow I'll make it on my three-day pass, which is coming up.

If a guy got an invite, he had to bring a girl. Male homos were barred but lesbians were welcome. Few men brought their wives or their close girl friends. In most cases your date was like a ticket to get in, hoping you might do better after you got there.

Here is the topper to the story that *Confidential Magazine* didn't know about. The late Irving Hoffman, erudite PR consultant to 20th Century-Fox and author of most of Walter Winchell's best-written columns, was a devout habitué of Dickenson's parties.

Hoffman would go to the Stork Club after the party and give Winchell a play-by-play account of the fun and games.

Walter was a pretty good player himself and Hoffman would have him drooling with his colorful account. Winchell kept figuring out how he could make the party, but he told Hoffman he was too recognizable and that too many people were out to hang him.

One night a Broadway actor is telling Winchell what a ball he had at Dickenson's. "And a funny thing, Walter," he says, "that guy Dickenson is a ringer for you. He could be your brother." Which was true, there was a strong resemblance at first glance.

Winchell chokes his rage and immediately gets Hoffman on the phone. Hoffman says he sounded like he was having apoplexy. "You never told me that dirty bastard looked like me," he screamed. "What dirty bastard?" Hoffman asked. "That son-of-a-bitch Dickenson. Now I'm the big joke around town."

Winchell found out when the soirée was scheduled, then contacted a couple of his detective friends from the 54th Precinct and told them there must be at least a half-dozen charges they could bust that joint for. He told them he wanted it raided.

Poor Walter Pidgeon was in the wrong place at the wrong time. It was the following week that he attended Dickenson's and that was the night the joint was raided. Dickenson and three other people were arrested, but the case seemed to fade away and no one heard much about it.

I wouldn't swear that Pidgeon hid his bare ass out on the window ledge, which was what the *Confidential* story was based on. I have a sneaking suspicion the cops let him off the hook.

Mike Todd, I

Dear Muffo:

Spent a couple of hours with Todd this afternoon, just the two of us. Cohn is off to the museum to check out some Hispanic lore for his *Don Quixote* project. Todd never mentions the five thousand and neither do I, but he does ask for you.

It's a real flashy apartment. He mixes me a scotch and soda, lights up one of his three dollar cigars and sits down opposite me. I notice him looking at my tie. It's a brocaded black-on-black job and my favorite. Suddenly he starts unknotting his tie. He takes it off and holds it out to me. It's a vomity green-brown. "I love your tie," he says. "Here, it's a trade." I know this bit. It's an old Broadway schtik. A kind of fraternal ceremony, swapping ties.

I say, "I don't want to trade, I like my tie." He's still holding out his tie and I can see he's a little pissed off. "For crissake, Conrad, you got no class. This tie is a Sulka." I say, "You got no taste. I wouldn't wear that tie to a cock fight."

"I got no taste? I got no taste?" Now he's sounding off. He's not looking at me. He's talking to the wall. "I win every award in the book for *Around the World* and this bum says I got no taste."

"Okay, so you got taste," I tell him, "but this tie is a present from my wife and I don't want to part with it."

He cools down and from the way he is looking at his tie I know he'll never wear that one again.

"Did Harrison tell you the story?"

I tell him, "No, he said you would, but I'm curious, Mike. What the hell are you doing screwing around with a lousy rag like *Confidential*? You're getting more ink than Eisenhower."

He blows some smoke rings and thinks a minute. "Couple of reasons," he says. "First, it makes me look like the nice guy I am." He does a comic "take." "And, second, I've been trying to stick it up Harry Cohn's ass for years. Oh, I got another reason. I got *Around the World* booked all over the country, which I expect you to mention. This guy's got six million circulation."

I find these valid reasons. "So what's the story?"

"This happened over three years ago, when I'm still concentrating on Broadway. Now this dame is not a bad actress. She had a seven-year contract at Columbia Pictures. She don't set the world on fire there the first two years and I get it straight that Cohn ain't going to pick up her option because her salary takes a pretty good jump."

"What's her name?" I ask. "Shut up and listen," he says. "Three days before her option is up I have my press agent, Bill Doll, put out a story that I am going to produce a drama starring this dame who has been under contract to Columbia Pictures. Sounds pretty good, a young movie actress getting the lead in a Broadway vehicle. The story gets a good play in the trades and theatrical sections. Now her option is up in three days.

"The next day I get a call from Harry Cohn. 'You ain't as dumb as I thought,' he says. 'That little girl is perfect for the part. If we can work out a little deal, I'll let you have her for a run-of-the-play contract.'

"I say, 'Harry, don't bullshit me. Her option is up in two days and I got it straight, you're not picking it up. I won't have to deal with you.'

"'That's not true,' he says, lying through his teeth. 'We love this kid here. We got big plans for her.'

"I say, 'That's great Harry, but I'm not going to talk deal on the phone. I'll be on the coast next week and we'll work it out.' He don't smell the rat.

"Then I call the dame's agent and tell him to stick by his phone because Cohn is going to call, which he does that afternoon. He picks up the option with some goodies thrown in."

"What was the play?" I ask.

"Some cockamamie thing I never intended doing, especially with this dame in the lead. Two days later I have Bill Doll put out another story. It says the author is making major revisions and the play is postponed indefinitely. Harry Cohn is no dummy. When he hears the play is postponed, he figures out the scam, but it is too late."

"You still haven't told me the dame's name," I say.

"I ain't going to tell you her name. You can't use it. I told that to Harrison."

"I don't give a shit, Mike," I say, "but it's only half a story without her name."

"Not my problem," he says. "Besides, the dame is still working in Hollywood and doing all right. Why make a *tsimiss* about it now?"

I have another drink and go home and knock out the piece in a couple of hours. I get some satisfaction out of it since Harry Cohn is the schmuck of the story and I think about the sweating I did when I worked at Columbia. God knows how those rascals will edit it, but who cares.

Sincerely,

Harold

Confidential Magazine, II

NEW YORK
NOVEMBER 1, 1957

Dear Muffo:

Don't know what kind of play the *Confidential Magazine* lawsuit is getting in the London papers. Since I got suckered into it, I better give you the details. At any rate I am now a pariah in my own home town.

For some time the Hollywood studios have been choking on every issue of Bob Harrison's sleazy rag. The Legion of Decency and the Bible Belt has been on their ass over the lurid revelations of their stars' life styles.

Since the heart of Harrison's operation is his Hollywood office, which operates under a phony name as a research organization, the Hollywood studio bosses got together and decided to sue him in California, where they have all the juice. They were confident they could destroy him.

Probably because of my own aberrations, I take a strong stand on the invasion of privacy and I think the suit is a good move. I call Bob Harrison to give him the needle, figuring he must be frantic. He isn't. He's ecstatic.

"I love it," he says. "I've already told my lawyers to be prepared to subpoena every big-name star who ever appeared in the magazine. Can you picture that parade up to the witness stand?"

"Do the Hollywood bosses know that?" I ask.

"They do now," he says. "The stars know the stories are true, for crissake. I got the affadavits. What are they going to do, perjure themselves?"

When the movie moguls realize the potential impact of Harrison's ploy, they reconvene. Harry Brand, the wise old public relations director at Fox who has spent half a lifetime covering up the peccadilloes of movie stars and probably figures the stories are true, tells the bosses it would be wise to call off the suit because it would only compound all the things Harrison has done to date. They agree to halt the legal proceedings and figure out another way to get Harrison.

Do you remember the famous Mary Astor divorce case some twenty years ago, which was smeared all over the front pages of the national press for a month? She had kept a diary in which she noted, in detail, her sex life, day by day including a list of her "ten top lovers." Leading the field by several lengths was George S. Kaufman, the famous playwright. The diary, which the press called "The Little Black Book," was introduced in evidence and caused a sensation. The judge in the case was a man named Goodwin Knight, who got enough publicity to pave the way to the governorship of California.

When the studio lawyers went to the presiding judge in the *Confidential* case and told him they wanted to halt proceedings, he told them no dice, that the law must have due process and the game was on. He remembered the Astor case.

The panic was on in Hollywood and suddenly none of the

big names in the sex stories were available, but a few of the witnesses called did appear. One of the biggest names to testify was our old buddy Mike Todd.

When asked how a man of his stature would have anything to do with a despicable publication like *Confidential,* since he was quoted directly throughout, he answered, "I never gave any story to *Confidential.* Some writer named Harold Conrad kept bothering me about a story he was doing for *Confidential.* I told him I didn't want to discuss it, but he said he was going to run the story anyway. I thought I better talk to him to protect myself." How do you like that for class, Muffo?

Since I was one of two of the only writers mentioned in the case, it was assumed that I was a key writer for *Confidential.* Overnight I became a leper, an outcast. Acquaintances shunned me and I even had a tough time convincing my friends. I was too embarrassed to walk into Toots Shor's, where a lot of my pals were good friends of the Hollywood people who had been smeared.

Jackie Gleason and I were friends way back when we had a tight clique at Toots Shor's and he used to let us sign the tabs for food and booze until we got the dough to pay up.

Several months ago *Confidential* ran a dopey piece on a party Gleason ran when he lived at the Astor. I was there. The magazine highlighted an incident about the late comedian Lew Parker crashing into a portable bar and smashing up the evening's liquor quota. The story made it look like a drunken orgy with inert bodies all over the floor.

The day my name was brought into the *Confidential* trial, Gleason figured I had to be the guy who wrote the story. He hasn't talked to me since.

Confidential also ran a piece on Dan Dailey, who was a big star at Fox. It was a story about Dailey's penchant for dressing up in women's clothes and had some homosexual overtones.

Dan and I had been good friends for years and we had worked together, but I only knew him as a big, tough harddrinking Irishman who had a long list of girl friends. He called me right after the trial, deeply hurt. Of course, he assumed I wrote the piece on him.

By now I'm fed up with this crucification. "How the hell would I know you're dressing up in your girl friend's clothes?" I yell over the phone, "And if I did, you know me well enough to know that I wouldn't write that crap."

I tell him the whole story and he understands and apologizes. Not many people do. But of all people you'd never figure Mike Todd to be that kind of a rat. Should I sue for perjury?

Sincerely,

Harold

Mike Todd, II

Dear Muffo:

Just hung up the phone after talking to Art Cohn on the coast. He's been heartsick over my *Confidential* debacle, since I'm his closest friend and he considers himself the instigator. Calls me a couple of times a week. Says he ducked Todd for several days after his miserable performance on the witness stand.

I keep asking him how Todd could do such a thing when he's always flaunting his class and he says Todd is strictly a street guy, "save yourself first."

I think he's getting fed up with Mike. They're flying in from the coast tonight. He's guest of honor at a Friars' dinner and he insists on schlepping Cohn with him. Cohn says he don't want to go, especially on that private plane Todd charters and gives the impression it's his plane.

Art's telling me, "I hate to fly in those little planes when you can get there faster and safer in a commercial plane. But you know Todd. That's his idea of class, your own plane that takes you where you want to go when you want to go."

Art says he's been trying to get Todd to cop some kind of plea with me, but he's too embarrassed to face me. At any rate, he says now, Mike is anxious to settle up the five thousand and will do it on this trip.

That's getting it the hard way.

Sincerely,

Harold

Crash

Dear Muffo:

It's six-thirty in the morning here. I am absolutely numb. I need somebody to talk to, but there's nobody here. Suddenly I find myself at the typewriter, writing to you although I am sure the news has already reached your desk, London time.

Ten minutes ago a friend on the AP desk here who knows I'm a good friend of Art's called. A small plane cracked up in a storm over New Mexico. Art Cohn and Mike Todd were killed instantly. I feel so helpless.

My first instinct is to call Marta, Art's widow, but it's only 3:30 A.M. in California. What if she hasn't been told? I couldn't bear to break the news to her.

I had so many things to say about Art, but the words won't come. And the irony for Todd, winding it all up in an unclassy place like Grant, New Mexico.

With heavy sadness,

Harold

Hemingway

Dear Muffo:

Mara just finished an engagement at the Americana in Miami Beach so we hop over here for a few days because this is where the action is. Castro has just marched into Havana in the final stage of his revolution which wins hands down, and the town has gone wild.

Alita Hernandez, a sharp dame from New York, is the press agent for the Havana Hilton. She gets us a beautiful suite in this brand-new hotel and she tells me Castro is my neighbor just above me and below is Jack Parr who came in with a TV crew to interview him.

What impresses me is how sure Castro is of himself. His personal security is practically nil although he moves some of the mountain troops who fought with him into the Hilton, but they're not guarding anybody, they're just on holiday. A lot of these guys have never been in a big city before. Alita tells me it is very hard for the most of them to believe that the beautiful toilet bowls were invented for what they're supposed to be used for.

The lobby is filled with soldiers, and they're a scroungy-looking bunch. The dummies don't have their safety catches on, one of them accidentally drops his gun on the marble floor, a mirror gets shot out and the clerk almost gets his hair parted.

The next day we go to the square to hear Castro make his big victory speech and it's an awesome sight. There must be a hundred thousand people jammed into the square. He's rattling away and waving his arms and after the first hour I grab Mara's arm and we cut out, but it seems like everybody else stays huddled in the hot sun and he speaks two hours more.

That night we make the rounds, the tourist spots like Sloppy Joe's and some of the in places, where I run into a few Cubans I know from past visits. They're well-to-do citizens who thrived under Batista and they're scared to death. They keep repeating an expression, "up against the wall." They say Castro is a Communist and they're planning to get out of Cuba right away or it's "up against the wall" for them.

I tell them they're overreacting, that everything seems to be under control and that Castro's no Communist. Matthews, the New York Times correspondent, says he isn't, and he spends a lot of time with Castro; but they just look at me like I'm some prize sucker.

I tell Mara we got to find Hemingway because we're leaving tomorrow. Now I'm not that great a buddy of Hemingway's but I drink with him in Madrid and at Toots Shor's and the last time I see him is in Havana with Mark Hellinger and Al Hershkovits, who came over to set up a movie deal. He knows who I am and he always seems glad to see me because I listen to him like he's a fight expert which he isn't really. He never gets out of the Dempsey era.

It's not hard to find Hemingway in Havana. His base when he is in town is the Floridita, where the frozen daiquiri was invented. When we get to the joint he's sitting at a table with Ken Tynan. Now I'm thinking, what the hell am I going to call Hemingway? I always have trouble with this. I called him Pops once and his glare was like a laser beam. Ernie he hates, Poppa he likes now, but I seem to have trouble saying "Poppa."

Mara and I are at the bar inhaling a couple of frozen daiquiris when he spots me. He comes over and gives me a big hello. I introduce him to Mara as Mr. Hemingway. He sucks in his gut, stands straighter and turns on the charm. He asks about what's going on back at Toots Shor's. I tell him how everybody was saddened over the death of Bill Corum. The popular Hearst sports columnist was a close friend of his. Then I start to tell him about all our mutual friends who were at the funeral. He holds up a finger and in an eerie tone, like a narrator for a ghost story, he says, "We don't talk about death or funerals." I get the message quick and change the subject.

Now as I look at him I realize he's gotten a lot older-looking than he should have gotten since I saw him last. We have another round of drinks and he says he better get back to Tynan.

"When are you going back?" he asks. I tell him three tomorrow afternoon. "Maybe I'll catch you before you leave," he says, but don't say when or where.

The next morning we have a couple of hours to kill so Mara and I go down to the lobby. It's almost deserted, except for some tourists. I don't know where the hell the soldiers have gone. As we cut across the lobby I see Hemingway coming toward us. "Just called your room," he says. "Thought we ought to have a farewell drink."

As we walk toward the bar he's talking to Mara, and I size him up. He's wearing a safari jacket and his famous barrel chest has slipped down into a heavy stomach. His beard is practically white and his eyes have lost that sparkle. "What the hell," I tell myself, "he's no kid." But with guys like Hemingway you have an indelible picture of them in your mind and it's always their best portrait. It makes me a little sad looking at him.

It's eleven-thirty in the morning when we're at the bar. He orders a Cuban coffee and brandy. There's a big tumult in the dining room just behind the bar and the bartender tells us Castro is in there.

A few minutes later Alita, the press agent, is coming toward us and she's got a guy in uniform with her. She introduces him as an aide to Castro and he tells Hemingway that Castro says he would be honored if he would have coffee with him and he is looking forward to meeting him.

Hemingway is silent for a few seconds. He picks up his demitasse cup, takes a sip of coffee, slowly puts it down and says, "You tell him I would be honored, too, but not at this time."

His answer rocks the aide more than a little bit. He mumbles something, backs off and they leave.

"How come?" I asked. "How come you brushed the No. 1 man in the country when he's trying to be friendly?"

"I'm an expert on revolutions," he says. "In six months, maybe a year he'll be gone and I'll still be here. I just don't want to get involved unless I have to."

We have another round of drinks and he says he has to get home. We shake hands goodbye in the middle of the lobby and leave him standing there. As we walk back to the elevator bank we keep watching and he's still standing there while the tourists ogle him. When he sees them looking at him he sucks in his gut, stands up straight and holds his head erect and you can see it's a chore.

I don't know why I make such a big thing of this. Most of us reach a stage in life where we start trying to con Father Time and some of us do better than others, but I'm afraid Hemingway's losing to the old man with the scythe, hands down.

Regards,

Harold

Joe Louis, I

Dear Muffo:

Just had lunch with two unlikely guests, and watching them in warm, friendly conversation takes me back in retrospect some twenty-three years to a night in Yankee Stadium when the honor of the free world was at stake and their meeting was not so cordial.

It was a night of hatred and atonement and there were wild cries like "kill the Nazi bastard" and "fuck Hitler." Now they are good friends and see each other from time to time.

Joe Louis and Max Schmeling are here with me to shill for the upcoming Patterson-Johansson fight, which we are doing in the Miami Beach Convention Hall, March 13th. It is not my idea to unite Louis and Schmeling down here and things are not working out too well, as I anticipated.

Max goes down to Miami Beach twice to watch Patterson train and the fans boo the shit out of him. As you well know Miami Beach is like a suburb of Tel Aviv and sending Schmeling down there is like sending Dr. Goebbels to Israel to publicize a soccer match.

I know you rarely meet a German who admits he was a Nazi and Schmeling doesn't either, but he has a case. When

121

it meant the concentration camp for consorting with Jews, Schmeling stuck his neck out for his Jewish fight manager, Yussel Jacobs. Paul Damski, his current business manager who is here with him, is a Jew.

But this is not what I want to get off my chest. As I told you, we have lunch this afternoon, but we have it in Joe Louis' room. I make a reservation early for the dining room and tell them Schmeling and Louis will be with me. While I'm having a cup of coffee, Maurie Frank, a decent man and a fine host and owner of this whole establishment, joins me.

I can see he is flustered. "You could do me a big favor and have lunch in Joe's room this afternoon."

"Why are you telling me to have lunch in Joe's room?" I ask like an idiot.

"You're in the Deep South, man," he says. "This is a white man's hotel. I've already made a concession giving Joe a room here, but it would save a lot of embarrassment if you didn't bring him into the dining room."

"What the hell do you mean, save embarrassment," I say. "I'm already embarrassed. I'm shocked. Are you telling me Joe Louis isn't good enough to eat in your dining room?"

"This has nothing to do with Joe Louis personally," he says. "It's the code. It's the way of life. If I start breaking the rules, I won't be in business long. Joe understands. He's been here a couple of days and you've never seen him in the dining room."

That point had never occurred to me. Of course I knew about segregation, but now I feel ashamed that I had to be touched by it to fully realize what a degrading, despicable thing this must be to the black man. I tell Mr. Frank where he can stick his dining room and start over to Joe's room.

On the way I run into Whitey Bimstein, one of the all-time great fight trainers. He is working here with Johansson. I tell him what's happening.

"A Nazi they'll let into the dining room," he says without taking the cigar out of his mouth, "but a great American like Joe Louis, they don't want him in there." In that second I wondered whether Louis really won the night he knocked out Schmeling.

When I get to Joe's I tell him we are going to have lunch in his room and that Schmeling will be over at twelve-thirty. He says, "Good." The phone rings and he answers it. It's for me. It's Maurie Frank, the owner.

"I've been thinking this thing over," he says. "Forget everything I said. Bring Joe in for lunch and the hell with anybody who doesn't like it."

I hang up and tell Joe it was Mr. Frank and the plans are now switched. We'll have lunch in the dining room.

Joe gives me a strange look. "You ask him 'bout us eatin' there?" I tell him I did.

"You shouldn't'a done that," he says. "You shouldn't'a done that." I can see his anger is smoldering. It's the first time I see Joe angry, in or out of the ring, except the night with Schmeling.

"You should'a know better," he's saying. "I don't want nobody begging for me to eat in a white man's place. I don't go where I'm not wanted." And that's how we come to have lunch in Joe's room.

Yesterday we take Johansson down to Miami Beach to work out. It's a hype for the fight. They haven't seen him down there yet. But we don't have a sparring partner for him. Whitey and I find Angelo Dundee and ask him if he's got a heavyweight Johansson can spar with.

"I got a kid who's only had four pro fights but he'll give the

Swede a good workout." Then he yells, "Hey Cash, get your ass over here," and this handsome six-foot-four Adonis bounces over. Angelo introduces him. He has the dubious name of Cassius Clay and now I recognize him as the kid who made all that noise in the Olympics. Angelo says, "Wanna' go three rounds with the Swede?"

Clay looks at Bimstein, then me. He is straight-faced but those big eyes seem to be laughing. Then in sing-song he says, "Do ah wanna go three rounds with the Swede, do ah wanna go three rounds with the Swede? Ahm gonna' be dancin' with Ingemar Johansson, ahm gonna' be dancin' with Ingemar Johansson, ahm gonna' be dancin' with Ingemar Johansson."

I look at Angelo. "What the hell was that all about?" I ask. "Oh, you haven't met this nut," he says. "You ain't heard nothin' yet."

Johansson never had too much to start with. He's got two left feet but a dangerous right hand (if he hits you with it) and he's got no sense of humor once he puts the gloves on. I'm afraid he's liable to punch some holes in this kid if he gets out of line.

Clay musta hit Johansson a half-dozen good left jabs in the first minute of the workout. It's the kind of jab that makes you sit up and pay attention. The Swede keeps plodding after him and whenever he tries to cut the ring off, Clay dances around him like he's Fred Astaire.

Johansson is furious between rounds and tells Bimstein he is going to flatten this fresh kid. But the second round is worse than the first. Ingemar completely blows his cool and goes chasing Clay with that right cocked. Whenever he throws it he misses by two feet. He hasn't hit Clay a punch yet.

Meanwhile Clay don't shut up. He's saying things like "I should be fighting Patterson, not you, sucker. I'm the next heavyweight champion of the world. Here I am, sucker. Come and get me, sucker."

Bimstein is so exasperated he calls off the workout after the second round and Johansson goes back to Palm Beach with a new neurosis.

This kid Clay fights as good as he talks. I'd like to see what happens when he gets hit on the chin, but I don't think that's going to happen often. His reflexes are fantastic. I think what we have here is a future heavyweight champion of the world.

Sincerely,

Harold

Six-Day Bike Race, I

NEW YORK
SEPTEMBER 2, 1961

Dear Muffo:

Remember the crazy six-day bike race? Well, they're reviving it after twenty-two years and the backers have made a very wise choice and hired me as the press consultant. The last six-day race was held in the Garden in 1939 when the war cancelled it out since ninety percent of the riders were European. I covered that last one for a couple of nights and to this day I haven't figured out what the hell was going on. It was the wildest event I ever saw at the Garden.

Just conjure up this bizarre picture, a bunch of guys continuously riding bicycles around a wooden track for six days and seven nights. If they were going someplace they could damn near get to Hollywood because they cover almost 2,600 miles.

I'm racking my brain for some kind of motive for the publicity campaign and I get an idea when I'm walking up Broadway last night. The marquee on the Latin Quarter says, "Sophie Tucker, in her farewell appearance." I did a piece on Sophie a few years ago and I remember her telling me she used to plug songs at the six-day bike race. I figure I'd get her to start the race, which has always been a big ceremony.

Maybe I can give this whole thing a Mauve Decade flavor because that's when the race was really in its heyday, so I do a little researching. In those days it was held in the old Garden down on 23rd Street. For a buck and a half you could go to the race and stay there for five days. They cleaned it out for the sixth day. It was cheaper than the Mills Hotel for the bums and it was Mecca for the pickpockets and hustlers.

The thieves would take anything that wasn't nailed down and if you saw some guy walking down the street in his bare feet you knew he just came from the bike race. It was a mistake to sit on your coat. If you got up to root during the race some bandit would scoop up your coat along with your neighbor's, rush back to the windows and drop them to a confederate waiting down in the street.

But the race had it's classy side and was an "in" thing for the Broadway show people because no matter what time they got to the Garden they could catch some action. The final sprints went off at four-thirty A.M. Flo Ziegfeld would take a box for the whole week and drape it with his famous beauties, the champagne flowed, and mobsters like Dutch Schultz and Jack (Legs) Diamond would challenge each other to see who would put up the most prize money for the sprints.

Then there were the song pluggers. Before radio and television music publishers had to get their songs sung in public places for exposure and the six-day race was the perfect set up. As a music maven you might be interested to know that two solid old standards, "Peg o'My Heart" and "For Me and My Gal," were first introduced at Garden races.

I really hope this thing makes it, and not just for personal reasons. It just seems a damn shame that two generations have grown up barely ever hearing about this crazy, happy event that used to come to town twice a year.

Anyhow I think it's going to be a lot of fun. I'm going to talk to Sophie tomorrow and I'm sure she'll go for it. If you were here I'd get you the pickpocket concession.

Regards,

Harold

Six-Day Bike Race, II

New York
September 19, 1961

Dear Muffo:

This bike race thing is really coming together. Advance sale's only been fair, but the press is enthusiastic and once we open I'm sure it will take off. See Sophie Tucker last week. Catch her in her dressing room right after she finishes her act.

"The Last of the Red Hot Mamas" is laid out on a divan, bundled in a robe with a towel around her neck. She points to a stool and motions for me to move it closer to the divan.

"I must look like a zombie," she says. "Just got off the stage a few minutes ago. God was it hot, but I really killed 'em. Three encores. Then I had to come straight in here and lay out before I did another thing. The old bones ain't what they used to be. Know what I mean?"

She still has all the make-up on, gobs of it. She has sequins on her eyelids, her long phony eyelashes look like a spider's nest and the mascara is tracing the crags of her great wrinkled face in little streams of sweat. But if she was thirty years younger she wouldn't have looked any better with all that crap on her face. She's in her seventies, you know.

Now I tell her about the bike race and ask her if she'd be

the honorary starter. "Love it, love it, Sonny-boy," she says, "and I'm not working that week. I'm a six-day bike race degenerate. Watched them races for over thirty years."

"What's the biggest thrill you ever got at a six-day race?" I ask.

"That's an easy one, Sonny-boy. It was the night I met Enrico Caruso at the Garden. Think it was in '16 or was it '17? Now there was a star. Hear what I'm telling you? What a talent! What a man! He could'a parked his shoes under my bed any night. And he was a genuine six-day bike race nut. Use to come to root for them paisanos from Italy and would go for five, six hundred a night putting up prize money for the sprints."

As I'm listening to her delivery it sounds very familiar; then it hits me. She sounds just like Mae West. Actually, I think she was doing Mae West before Mae West. So everything is moving along fine. A guy named Jimmy Prochia is putting this whole thing together. He's a zany kind of a guy who figures to be tied up in a six-day bike race. He works for the Sanitation Department as an inspector, but when he works I don't know because he's been tied up on this thing, night and day, for a month. Anytime I see any garbage on the street I blame him.

For the last ten days he's been down in the Madison Square Garden basement with twenty carpenters, putting the track together in sections. On the morning of the race they'll move all of the sections up to the main floor and hook 'em up. It's tricky. The track has to be calibrated perfectly, the straightaway canting to an angle of 25 degrees and the turns to an angle of 48 degrees.

The riders are all in town and there are fifteen teams from

twelve different countries. They're a whacky bunch of guys, which figures, but they're superbly trained athletes. This racket requires as much guts and stamina as the toughest of sports.

One of the best bets of the race is going to be the food. Leone's Restaurant is doing the catering. The press gets to eat with the riders and the restaurant is open twenty-four hours a day. When I covered the race, years ago, everybody in the sports department got to go at least once, just for a shot at the food. It was better than the best restaurant in town.

Keep your fingers crossed, Muffo. I think we got a winner here.

Regards,

Harold

Six-Day Bike Race, III

NEW YORK
SEPTEMBER 22, 1961

Dear Muffo:

Le Six Jour est mort.

Those are not my words. This Gallic mouthful came from André Retrain, one of the French riders, and I think he knows what he's talking about. What happened here last night was incredible.

The race is scheduled to kick off at nine o'clock. I get to the Garden about eight and the upper balcony is already three-quarters filled. The track looks beautiful although there are still some gaps to be connected. They've hired twenty more carpenters and now they've got forty guys banging away with hammers. We've got less than an hour to go and I'm not worried about the gaps. With all those hammers they should be able to build Noah's Ark in less time than that.

I go to the restaurant, which is packed with free-loaders, and have a couple of drinks. When I get back to the track it is eight-forty-five and I notice that not only are the gaps still there, but men are ripping sections out of the opposite ends of the track. Prochia is running around like a madman, yelling at the carpenters. I ask Alf Goullet, the chief referee, what the hell is going on.

135

"Big trouble," he says. "You wouldn't believe."

"Believe what?" I asked.

"Twenty years ago somebody gave Prochia the plans for the Garden floor, but they were for the old Garden downtown and he didn't know the difference. Those plans have got to be eighty years old and that's what he's been working off. Would you believe that?"

"What the hell are we going to do?" I ask.

"We got the differences figured out. Now it's just a matter of time."

Just then I notice Sophie taking her seat in the box and I'm wondering whether I ought to go see her or take off for Brazil. She's wearing a large picture hat and a gown right out of the Mauve Decade. She looks great.

There are about 12,000 people in the joint and they're beginning to get a bit testy. The forty carpenters are hammering away like mad. They sound like the Anvil Chorus; and Basile's band is gallantly trying to play, "Yes, Sir, That's My Baby," but it don't stand a chance.

Now it's past eleven and people are starting to leave. By eleven-thirty we have half a house, but the restaurant is doing an SRO business and the free-loaders are lined up out into the hall. The press room has put out a call for more booze.

Past midnight the crowd is strangely silent. They just sit there mesmerized, watching those forty carpenters drive in the nails like it was part of the show. Finally word is passed around that the race will start at one A.M.

At a quarter-to-one all the carpenters leave the track and a lone rider appears. He circles the track once, twice, three times, taking all the banks, high and low. Then he raises his hand, thumb upturned. It's okay. The crowd, or what's left of it, lets out a roar and everybody comes back to life.

I go up to get Sophie and "The Last of the Red Hot Mamas" is fast asleep. Her hat is askew, her shoes are off and the mascara is trickling down her cheek. I nudge her gently and she opens her eyes.

It's a pretty good walk down to the starting line so I say, "Sophie, it's very late. If you'd rather sit here and take a bow that would be fine."

"Nothing doing, Sonny-boy. I told you I was gonna do it and I'm gonna do it." She takes out a mirror, straightens her hat and repairs her face. Getting her shoes on is a major operation. Finally we walk slowly down to the starting line. The gun goes off, Sophie cuts the tape and the 75th International Six-Day Bike Race is off on its mad dash to nowhere.

But I'll tell you something, Muffo. The Frenchman was right. *Le Six Jour est mort.*

Regards,

Harold

Luciano, II

Dear Muffo:

Remember me telling you about a Florentine silver ciga-rette case Lucky Luciano gives me? That's four years ago. Yesterday I ask Mara what ever happened to the case. "It's around someplace," she says.

Why I ask about the case at this time I have no idea. This morning I see the case on my desk. Mara finds it and leaves it for me. I look it over and it's really worth admiring. Then I turn to my copy of the *New York Times* and on the obit page there is a story out of Naples that for this particular moment is an eye-popper for me.

Luciano dies of an apparent heart attack at Capodichino Airport while under surveillance by Italian and United States authorities who are about to arrest him as boss of an international narcotics network.

I get a picture of Lucky, standing on his Bay of Naples terrace, protesting because he is being fingered as a dope runner. And I remember his last words. "Tell Georgie I want to get in the movies one way or another."

When they roll his body over at the Naples Airport they

see he's laying on a movie script titled *The Luciano Story,* a screen treatment.

Pardon the pun, but you might call this falling into the movie business the hard way.

Regards,

Harold

A. J. Liebling

Dear Muffo:

The damndest thing happened yesterday and I know you'll be interested because it concerns A. J. Liebling, who wrote your favorite fight book, *The Sweet Science.*

I'd seen Joe Liebling around the fight ringsides for years and when you meet him you figure he'd be the last guy in the world to get hung on the fight racket. He's a soft-spoken, unassuming man, squat and rolypoly, and he shuffles around like a walking Buddha.

We're putting together the first Patterson-Liston fight and it's scheduled for Yankee Stadium in New York later in the year. The other day I get a call from Liebling. He respect-fully asks if it would be possible for him to meet Liston. He'd like to do a piece on him. I tell him no problem—that I'm going up to check out Liston's training camp on Thursday if he wants to come. He's delighted.

On Thursday we drive up to The Pines where Sonny has just started training. It's one of those lush Borscht Circuit joints in the heart of the Catskills. Sonny just walks into the gym about the time we get there. The workout is closed to the public.

I go over to Sonny and tell him who Liebling is while Joe hovers meekly in the background, then I call him and he shuffles over in his slow, painful gait. Liston shoves his big paw out and Liebling sticks his head back to look up at him as they shake. Sonny studies him for a few seconds, then looks at me and smiles.

Now Sonny climbs into the ring and belts the bejesus out of a couple of sparring partners. Liebling is watching from a chair they place at ringside for him. When he's finished in the ring, Sonny sets a towel over his head and puts on a terry cloth robe. The sweat is pouring out of him. As he slowly walks around the floor drying out, he calls me.

"Ask your fat friend if he wants a cup of tea," he says.

I ask Liebling and he says he'd love one, so Joe Palino, one of the trainers, brings him the tea and he sits there with it on his lap. Suddenly Liston starts yelling at Palino.

"I ain't gonna' give you the five bucks, you cheap muzzler," says Liston. "You better give me the five," says Palino. "Not if you live to be a hundred," says Liston.

"Zat so," says Palino and he backhands Liston across the shoulder. With that, Liston reaches into the pocket of his robe and hauls out a small revolver and aims it at Palino, who runs over to where Liebling is sitting and kneels right behind him. I can see the fright in Liebling's eyes even through his thick lenses.

Liston extends his arm and takes dead aim right at where Liebling is sitting with Palino hiding behind. Then "bang!" The gun goes off. It's a blank of course, but Liebling goes over backwards, the cup goes up in the air and the tea drenches him. Sonny is stamping his foot and laughing hysterically, an exercise he don't often indulge in.

When I go over to Liebling he's still shaking. I'm embarrassed to death for him, but he brushes the whole thing off like he was happy to be a part of a training camp prank even if he was the mark.

On the drive back I ask Joe what went through his mind when he saw Liston aim the gun in his direction. "Well, I had read all about his prison record and I bought it," he says. "I was just praying he had good aim."

To tell you the truth, Muffo, I think Liston took a year off Liebling's life that afternoon.

Regards,

Harold

(top) The man in the center is Muffo, otherwise known as Bob Musel, UPI's legendary roving correspondent and long time friend of Harold Conrad. The man attached to the finger at the right is Earl Wilson.

(left) Harold Conrad with superstar Al Jolson and Henry Armstrong, who held three world's boxing titles at the same time. Jolson allegedly owned Armstrong—nobody owned Conrad.

On the town in 1947. Georgie Woods with Joe Adonis's nose; one of the lovelies from the Colonial Inn nightclub; and Harold Conrad.

Mara Lynn

The youngest boxing writer on the beat, Harold Conrad, being held in check by Max Baer, who had just won the title from Primo Carnera.

Ham Fisher didn't like to pay in cash.

Joe Louis and Max Schmeling 23 years after their epoch fight. That's Conrad in the middle as usual.

Two youngsters: Joe Louis, who had just won the heavyweight title from Jimmy Braddock, and pal Harold Conrad who wrote about it.

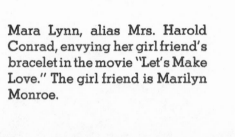

Mara Lynn, alias Mrs. Harold Conrad, envying her girl friend's bracelet in the movie "Let's Make Love." The girl friend is Marilyn Monroe.

Mara and Harold in front of their honeymoon cottage in the
Canyon, twenty minutes from the Polo Lounge.

Training for the second Liston fight, Conrad on the right with pals Buddy Hackett and Robert Ryan.

At Toots Shor's, the eventful collaboration of Marianne Moore and Muhammad Ali on the poem rescued from the kitchen by George Plimpton.

(bottom) In Dublin, Muhammad Ali, Conrad, and John Huston—an old four round fighter who went into the movie business.

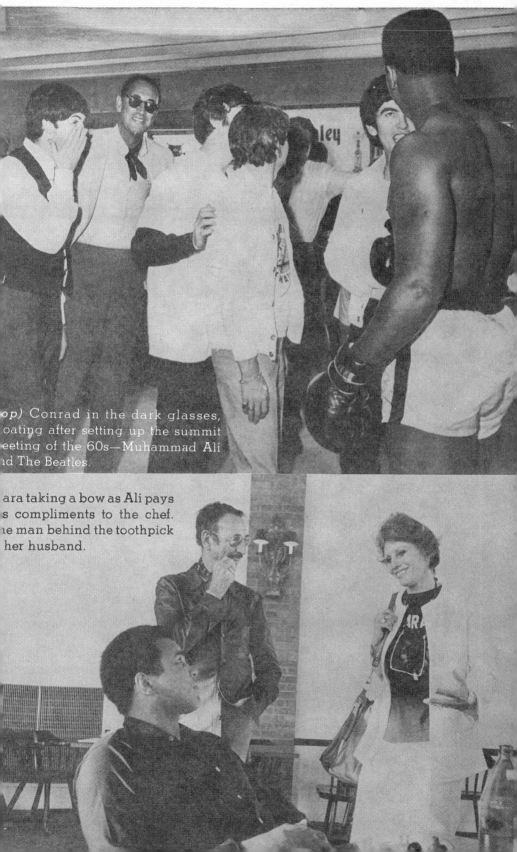

op) Conrad in the dark glasses,
oating after setting up the summit
eeting of the 60s—Muhammad Ali
id The Beatles.

ara taking a bow as Ali pays
s compliments to the chef.
e man behind the toothpick
her husband.

Harold Conrad being toasted by shipmates aboard the *France*, enroute from Cherbourgh to New York. That's Conrad making a move to get up and take a bow.

Harold Conrad with Lady Remington aboard the *Queen Mary*, enroute from Southampton to New York.

(top) For the 1948 Olympics, Ted Husing, Harold Conrad, and J. Arthur Rank's producer, Castleton Knight.

(right) Harold Conrad on the road with Sonny Liston. Conrad is running to keep up with Liston's walk.

Left, Harold Conrad, right, Budd Schulberg, and, separating them, Ferdi Macheco, M.D., the fight doctor.

Harold Conrad, left, Al Capp, right, with an unidentified man in the middle.

Conrad pondering a Budd Schulberg question at Ali's training camp.

Up in the rocket is Evel Knievel. Down below, Harold Conrad acting like he knows what he is doing.

Chicago, I

Dear Muffo:

Looks like we finally get the Liston-Patterson fight together, and it may be the hottest heavyweight fight in years. It's all set for Comisky Park here in Chicago, September 25th. It is supposed to be in New York and we even have a deposit down on Yankee Stadium for September, but the New York State Boxing Commission pulls a switch the last minute and refuses to license Sonny.

Mayor Wagner grabs me last week and he's crying the blues over New York blowing the fight, says it will cost the city five million in hotel, food, and entertainment revenue. I tell him to talk to Rockefeller. It was his office that pulled the rug from under the Commission.

The cast of characters on the fight scene is changed the past year. Derbies and cigars are out and tweeds and pipes are in. Roy Cohn, the lawyer, is the man behind the stick. Tom Bolan, his law partner, is president of Feature Sports. A stockbroker named Fred Brooks and Bill Fugazy, the travel bureau mogul, are on the edges someplace, although Brooks claims he's the boss. Not long ago Fugazy smashes

Brooks over the head with his attaché case so things haven't changed all the much.

There's some corporate finagling going on. Three guys named Graff, Reiner and Smith are heading up the closed-circuit company. I don't mind that none of these guys know a left hook from a kick in the nuts, but running a closed circuit is a sophisticated operation. These suckers haven't the slightest idea what's going on and I'm not going to have time to educate them. In addition to the live gate at Comisky Park, we're going to have a half-million seats available in theaters around the country and it's my job to see that there are asses in those seats.

Yesterday Al Bolan, my partner, who is Tom's brother, went to see Mayor Daly with me. Usually, if you want to put a big fight on and you go over the Commission's head, you appeal to the governor. But, in Chicago, Daly's the boss and he doesn't bother about commissions. I suspect Cohn already has the deal wrapped up with Daly and our meeting is brief.

Daly could be a movie mayor in his beautifully tailored suit with white carnation in buttonhole and he has that fresh-out-of-the-chair look, a matte of white talc on pink jowls. "So you want to put the Patterson-Liston fight on here," he says.

"Yes, Your Honor," I tell him. "It will bring millions of dollars into Chicago"; and I'm just getting wound up to give him my spiel when he stops me.

"Never mind all that," he says. "I just want to know one thing. Is this going to be a good fight? I don't want this town's image loused up."

I look him straight in the eye. "Your Honor," I say, "this is going to be one of the greatest fights of all times."

If I'm wrong he can call me pisher.

Regards,

Harold

Chicago, II

Dear Muffo:

The fight's less than a week off and we're rolling pretty good. Looks like it's going to be a big winner on closed circuit. Got the best setup I ever have thanks to Margie Abrams, the town's No. 1 press agent. The Sheraton is press headquarters and she gets me a penthouse suite you wouldn't believe. Got one of the main ballrooms for the working press base, with a couple a hundred typewriters, all the communication facilities and a twenty-four-hour bar. We'll have close to six hundred newspapermen here by fight time.

Then there's the authors, Norman Mailer, Budd Schulberg, James Baldwin, A. J. Liebling, Nelson Algren, and Gerald Kersh, with more coming and they're all on assignment to cover the fight. Kersh, the British author, is really something. You read his novel, *Night in the City.* Hell of a book.

Kersh, who used to be a wrestler, goes around bending dimes with his teeth. He's the No. 1 sucker in the nightly poker games. He has a big vein in the center of his forehead and every time he tries to bluff his way through a big pot the vein sticks out like a neon sign. He's getting murdered and nobody will tip him off.

Liston and Patterson aren't the only guys training here. Mailer is in training, too. He's training for his big debate with William Buckley, which takes place here the night before the fight; and if boozing is the way you train for a debate Norman wins this one hands down. Lot of interest in the debate. It's like the semifinal to the main event.

Couldn't get to sleep the other night. The most incredible thing happened earlier in the day. Al Bolan asks me if I know a make-up man. "A make-up man for what?" I ask.

"It's for Patterson," he says. "I don't know what the hell he's got in mind."

I know Patterson can get a little balmy at times so I don't ask any questions. I call a friend of mine at the local CBS TV station and make an appointment for him. My friend calls me back the next day after he's seen Floyd. "What the hell's playing with Patterson?" he asks. "He had my man fix him up a beard."

A beard is a disguise. Knowing Patterson's shyness and insecurity, I put two and two together. This guy is already planning what he's going to do if he loses. He's going to walk around with the beard figuring nobody will recognize him. I'm sure losing often crosses a fighter's mind, but to make definite plans *in case*? If you're going in to fight Liston with this negative frame of mind, forget it. I swear my friend at CBS into secrecy because the implications are scary. Right now this fight is almost even in the betting and that's why it's such a hot ticket. If it gets out, the whole picture could change. It's a hell of a story but I got to sit on it.

If I was a betting man I'd bet the family jewels on Liston.

Regards,
Harold

Chicago, III

Dear Muffo:

We're forty-eight hours away from post time and this town is really jumping. Did I tell you I bring Jack Kearns in as a kind of conversation piece? I figure Jack Dempsey's flamboyant old manager would add a little color to the promotion just sitting around talking to the press guys.

I call Kearns the other day and tell him I'll pay his expenses and give him five hundred pocket money if he wants to come in for the fight. All he has to do is shake some hands and buy a few drinks. Last night Kearns is down in the Grill with a dozen of his old cronies. He don't want to drink up in the press room where the booze is on the cuff and he's buying champagne with my pencil. He spends more in one night than I spend in a week.

I get a wire yesterday morning which reads, "Know it's late but it's imperative I get credentials to cover the fight." It's signed, "Ben Hecht." It's way past the deadline, but am I going to turn down Ben Hecht? I read every book he writes; so I wire back a confirmation.

I go down to the press room this afternoon and there's a guy at a center table beating hell out of a typewriter. He's got his hat down over his eyes, his collar open and a cigarette dangling from his lips. A group of young sportswriters is lined up against the wall watching him. I see it's Ben Hecht. I walk over to him and notice he's finishing a page of neatly typed lines, but as I look closer they all say, "Now is the time for all good men to come to the aid of their party." Hecht has just been doing a matinee for the young writers.

"You're just the guy I've been looking for," he says. "I need someone to tell me what the hell is going on here."

I'm wondering who he's covering for. I figure he's got a big deal with *Life* or *Look* so I ask him. He looks over his shoulder, then leans close to me and says, "I'm covering for this hometown paper, the *Hackensack News*. I've been reading in Leonard Lyon's column about all the authors here to cover the fight. I spent the best years of my young life here in Chicago as a newspaperman and I wasn't about to let those guys take over my town with a big story breaking. I had to be here."

I quickly overcome my surprise when Hecht tells me he is covering the fight for obscure *Hackensack News,* but I think you have to have been an ex-newspaperman to understand how he feels. Once you've been trained as a reporter, all news stories become your legacy no matter what other fields you may roam. The ink stains are figuratively like tattoos and cannot be removed. It's the long-distant whistle of the locomotive in the loneliness of the night that haunts the retired old engineer, envious because he is not at the throttle.

Everybody's in town now so I decide to have a little "in" party for some friends in the penthouse last night. I find out what I really need is a referee. I don't know why guys get rambunctious around a fight promotion. It's really contagious. Mailer, who is still in training for his debate tomorrow night, is drinking doubles. He gives Jimmy Baldwin a hard time and Jimmy runs out of the room close to tears.

I like Jimmy Baldwin and I'm delighted that he's around, but I'm still wondering what the hell he's doing covering a fight. He doesn't know a left hook from a kick in the ass and he thinks that the fight racket is a brutal business that should be abolished. But he has compensated for his emotions by viewing the fight as a battle between good and evil and he sees Patterson as the White Knight. I say "White Knight" because I don't want to louse up the vernacular. In Jimmy's book the Black Knight would be the White Knight.

Jimmy Cannon, the Hearst columnist, insults the hell out of Budd Schulberg. For good measure he adds some nasty things about Budd's father, B. P. Schulberg, the old Paramount picture boss, and Cannon isn't even drinking.

Gerald Kersh comes in with three hookers and Jack Cuddy, the United Press writer, throws a few verbal hooks at him. Kersh threatens to heave him off the terrace, which is only 42 stories up from the ground, and we have to untangle them.

Hecht gets good and mulled and goes on and on with old Chicago newspaper stories. Toward the end of the evening the only one listening to him is the bartender.

Jim Murray, the *Los Angeles Times* columnist, makes a sage comment. "I've heard a half-dozen beefs here tonight but nobody's mentioned anything about the big beef, the one we all came here to cover."

I realize Murray's right. Not one word has been said about the big fight. For some reason I'm offended, but what the hell, it will be all over in forty-eight hours.

Regards,

Harold

Norman Mailer

Dear Muffo:

Just got back from the big debate, Mailer vs. Buckley, and although Mailer is overtrained, I think he wins it by a hair. When the going gets tough, Buckley is tricky and verbose, like a guy holding on in the clinches. Norman goes straight for the jugular and I got to give it to him on aggressiveness.

The debate is held at the Medina Temple with big Irv Kupcinet as the moderator and, I must admit, that Mailer is a hot ticket. The joint is sold out and he's the big attraction. At least fifty of the visiting sports writers turn out for the word battle and the whole thing takes on the flavor of a big-time promotion with assorted booing and cheering.

Both protagonists come out cautiously throwing light literary jabs, but the pace picks up quickly and Norman throws a couple of round-house rights. When Bill tries to cut the ring off with a loquacious Bucklian riposte, Norman counters with, "Mr. Buckley, you want me to lie down on the railroad tracks, tie my hands to the rails and wait until the engine of your logic gets around to riding over me?" The Mailer cheering section loved that one.

Just made a hell of a deal with Hugh Hefner. That *Playboy*

Magazine of his is really starting to make big money. I tell him he should take advantage of the fact that many of the world's top newspaper men are here to cover the fight and that it would be a smart move if *Playboy* threw a big post-fight party at his mansion.

He agrees. I can invite two hundred and fifty and he'll invite one hundred and fifty. He'll take care of the tab. What could be fairer than that?

Got to sign off now. Tomorrow's the big day.

Regards,

Harold

158

Chicago, IV

Dear Muffo:

The fight grosses $4,000,600. I work on it for fourteen weeks and here I am sitting with about eight bucks in my pocket and a plane ticket back to New York. As you probably read, by order of the Attorney General's Office, the Feds not only grab the $625,000 live gate money, but all the dough in the 420 theater box offices around the country as well.

Scraped up enough dough to pay off the staff, but I owe the Hotel Sheraton $16,420.64, a debt I promptly reendorse to Roy Cohn's company, but I'm on my ass.

The Attorney General's office points out that there's a precedent for this snatch. They say that Johansson ran out of the country with all his dough from the third Patterson fight without paying his taxes and that fight guys can't be trusted anyhow.

That's all bullshit and not at all relevant. Johansson is a foreigner. We're all citizens and we're not about to run out of the country. The theater owners, who get to keep fifty percent of the take, scream bloody murder and they have been told that their fight money will be refunded immediately. But the promotion's money will be held and Uncle will take his cut out first, when he's ready.

Bobby Kennedy and Roy Cohn are counsel to Joe McCarthy during those miserable proceedings and the two of them are always beefing. According to rumor, they terminate their association with a fist fight. It's no secret that Bobby is out to get Cohn. Now he's Attorney General and all he has to do is pick up a phone. He did.

The whole thing's ludicrous. They have to put at least six hundred guys in the field to attach the theater box offices all over the country, at the taxpayers' expense, of course. I think this is pushing a grudge a little bit too far, don't you?

I don't even want to talk about the fight, but the party at Hefner's mansion is a smash. We're supposed to invite four hundred. Six hundred get in—movie stars, Bunnies, politicians, writers, hookers and I'm sure several goniffs.

There is action on all three floors with two bands, choice food and booze. It's a Bacchanalian orgy with drunks all over the place, including me, wild dancing, bare-breasted broads in the swimming pool and colorful reports of indiscriminate humping.

About five A.M. I run into Mailer. The party's going strong and he looks wild-eyed. "I want to talk to you," he says. His two hands are stuck in his jacket pockets and he stands there swaying, like the captain on the bridge of a wind-swept vessel. "I got something to say to the press and I want to talk to them," he says.

"Fine," I tell him. "Be in the press room on the fifth floor at ten A.M." It doesn't occur to me what the hell Norman's got to say to the press since I'm drunk as he is and I forget the whole thing.

The big press conference where Liston, the new heavyweight champion, is to be unveiled is scheduled for noon, but we push it back to ten o'clock because of the many different deadlines the press guys have around the world.

Incidentally, Patterson is nowhere to be found. I was right about the beard being a disguise. Not only did he have the beard going for him, but he had two waiting cars parked, one pointing to oblivion and one that would have led a victory parade. I guess he took the oblivion car.

The press conference is in the main ballroom and there's over three hundred newspapermen waiting to hear Liston's immortal words, but he's late. I run down to Liston's suite and he's just coming out, surrounded by a phalanx of tough-looking Chicago cops. We all head through a back door of the main ballroom and on to the wings of the stage.

As I look out on stage I do a double-take. Mailer is sitting right in the center of the dais, in Liston's seat. Liston looks out and like the big daddy bear says, "Who dat sittin' in mah chair?" A big cop says, "I'll get the son of a bitch out of there." Norman keeps sitting there, just staring out into space, oblivious to the one-liners the newspaper guys are throwing at him. He hasn't slept in two days and he's still drunk.

I tell the cops to hold everything a second and I'll get it straightened out. I go and talk to Norman. I beg him, I beseech him to get off the stage. He absolutely refuses. I tell him the cops are liable to work him over. He says, "Fuck the cops." The cops are watching my futile attempts and I can see they're already tasting Norman's blood.

A news photo flashes through my mind. It is a picture of a guy named Avery who refuses to leave a Montgomery Ward stockholders meeting and the cops just pick up the chair with him in it and carry him out. I go back to the wings. Now the cops are really out for Norman's ass. I tell them, "The world press is out there watching so don't fuck with this guy. Just pick up the chair and carry him off gently." They do just that and Norman rides out like a Chinese mandarin while the press corps cheers.

We're half-way through the press conference when there's a voice from the back of the room. It's Mailer again and there are shouts of "Throw the bum out," but Liston, an obstreperous boozer himself, has some empathy. "Leave the bum be," he says. "He's just drunk." We finally get the press conference over with and it winds up with Liston and Mailer shaking hands.

Just think, Muffo, fourteen weeks of hard work to build this thing up and the God-damned fight lasts two minutes and six seconds, with no payday yet. What a business.

Regards,

Harold

The Beatles

Dear Muffo:

A couple of burgeoning young phenomenas have taken over this town and they couldn't have a better stage. One is Cassius Clay, the overnight *wunderkind* of the boxing world and the other is a group called The Beatles who have upset the pop music world with a new sound that is particularly contagious to people under twenty-one. The older folks seem to be resisting it, but I find it getting to me.

All eyes seemed to be focused on this town with Clay getting ready to try and wrest the title from that big ugly bear, Sonny Liston. The Beatles are here for their second exposure to the American public on Ed Sullivan's TV show.

Despite the fact that Clay is an eight-to-one underdog in the betting, he is dominating the scene here, more with his mouth than his fists. We're almost up to the five hundred mark with newspapermen from all over the world and out of this whole crowd there's less than a half-dozen picking him to beat Liston, but they hang on his every word and can't seem to get enough of him.

It seems that this kid Clay can do almost anything he puts his mind to. I take him to Milton Berle's opening night show at the Eden Roc Hotel last week and as we sit watching the show Cassius says, "I can make a fortune doing what that Berle is doing." Then Milton calls him up on stage for an introduction and hits him with some funny lines.

Cassius holds his own fending them off. Then he asks Berle, "Are you a big star?" Milton says, "I'm the biggest." Then Clay asks, "How much these folks paying to see you here tonight?" Milton tells him the cover charge is twenty dollars.

Clay gives him one of his funny looks. "You work cheap," he says. "I guess I'm a bigger star than you are. They got to pay $250 for a ticket to my show." Then he jumps down off the stage, leaving Berle without an answer.

Cassius watches Leroy Neiman, the brilliant young artist, doing a sketch at the gym workout. The next day he presents Neiman with a sketch which he has just done, an intricate drawing of himself in the ring and the faces around ringside. It's not bad.

It doesn't take any genius to figure out that putting the Beatles together with Cassius Clay would make a picture that would be irresistible to most editors around the world. The man to see to get to the Beatles is a guy named Brian Epstein, who discovered them.

I spend a whole morning trying to track Epstein down, but he is unavailable. I finally grab him in the hotel lobby and introduce myself. I tell him I'd like to invite the boys to Clay's workout. He's facing me squarely, but his eyes are looking far away. He is on a magic carpet flying over Bombay at ten thousand feet.

After a long pause he mumbles, "Can't do it, man. Security." And that was that.

I have already arranged with Ed Sullivan for Liston to

take a bow on the show that is headlining the Beatles at the Deauville Hotel Sunday. Sonny and his wife, Jerry, are to meet me in the lobby a half-hour before show time. As I drive down Collins Avenue to the hotel, there's a line of people five blocks long hoping to get into the broadcast.

We have seats up front, and half-way through the show Sullivan introduces Sonny with a good plug for the fight. When the Beatles are introduced, I'm afraid the kids are going to take the joint apart.

About two minutes into their first number, Liston nudges me. "Fa' crissakes," he says, "is them bums what all this fuss is about? Sheet, man, mah dawg play better drums than that kid with the big nose."

I still haven't given up putting Cassius and the Beatles together and I go backstage after the show to see Sullivan. I ask him if there's any chance of me meeting the boys. He says, "Sure, I'm going up to the suite to see them now."

The hallway outside the suite is packed with photographers and squealing little girls, but security opens up a path for Sullivan. Inside, the boys are sitting quietly with a couple of British friends. They all jump up when Sullivan comes in.

"I want to thank you kids for a great show," Ed says in his inimitable fashion, "and I'd like you to meet an old friend, Harold Conrad. He's here doing the Liston-Clay fight."

I can see this ignites a spark. "Who's going to win?" Lennon asks.

"I like Cassius," says McCartney.

"Me, too," says Harrison.

I can see I have sympathetic ears. "How'd you guys like to see him work out?"

"Great, can we?" McCartney asks.

"How about tomorrow?" I say. "I'll arrange it, but I must tell you, I asked Brian Epstein about this and he said no soap." They all look at each other and Lennon says, "Don't worry about Brian, we'll handle him."

I say, "A man named Cole will pick you up here tomorrow at noon and he'll have plenty of security with him, but please don't say a word about this to anybody." One thing I didn't need was a horde of squealing kids taking up valuable press space.

I tip off Rocky Pomerantz, the Miami Beach chief of police, and wait until the last minute to let the wire service press photographers in on it. When the boys show up, Clay is already in the ring, shadow-boxing. When he finishes, I take them up into the ring and introduce them to Cassius.

Clay starts to upstage them and gives them weird looks. Then he says, "You guys are making a lot of money. You ain't as dumb as you look." The Beatles aren't sure how to take this crack. Then Lennon says, "But you are," and everybody laughs.

As they pose for the photographers, I watch this Summit meeting—The Beatles and Cassius Clay—the two hottest names in the news, worldwide. They are all about the same age. I wonder how posterity will treat them.

Sincerely,

Harold

Muhammad Ali, I

Dear Muffo:

Well, we got a new world's heavyweight champion and his name is Muhammad Ali. If you're wondering what happened to Cassius Clay, we buried him two weeks ago and it's been a weird two weeks. I'm director for the closed-circuit group that stages the Ali-Liston fight last night, but for a while there it looks like Cassius or Muhammad Ali isn't going to get that title shot because there isn't going to be any fight.

A guy named Bill MacDonald who makes a fortune down here in real estate is the local promoter. He outbids Las Vegas with an offer of $625,000 for the live gate and he is co-promoting it at the Miami Beach Auditorium with Chris Dundee. Everything is moving along fine until two weeks ago when MacDonald calls me in.

"I hear some disturbing news," he tells me. "I hear that Cassius is becoming a Muslim."

"That's hard to believe," I say. "The Muslims are a very strict, orthodox sect. I just don't think it's his style, Bill. He's too much of a free soul."

The next day I go out to the little house where Cassius is

staying in South Miami, and I notice a new set of guys around him. They're an unsmiling, unfriendly bunch. They're all wearing black suits and black ties and their hair is cropped short.

When I ask where Cassius is one of the brothers says, "You can't see him, he's busy." He's a bit nasty and I note that all the faces are hostile. It's getting scary. I tell him it's important that I see Cassius right away and he says, "Just wait out there on the porch." I wait more than an hour and Cassius finally comes out. He's with Malcolm X, who is his indoctrinator. I already met Malcolm. We once had a long discussion on the relativity of publicity and public relations. I find him bright and articulate.

Cassius gives me a cold hello like I'm some stranger. I tell him I have something important to discuss with him in private. He says there won't be any private discussions and now I realize the rumor MacDonald heard is true. A few days later Cassius makes a public announcement that he has become a Muslim and it shakes up everybody, including most of the blacks in the South who are having enough trouble as it is without some brothers calling the honkies "White Devils."

Cassius makes it clear that he is no longer to be called Cassius Clay and that from now on he will be known as Muhammad Ali. But Richard Durham, editor of *Muhammad Speaks,* the Muslim newspaper, tells me that Cassius is very unhappy when he is given his new name. He loves the name Cassius Clay, Jr., and makes a loud beef about the change, but he is finally convinced that Cassius Clay is a slave name and that Muhammad Ali is one of the most revered names in the Muslim sect.

MacDonald is sizzling and tells Cassius he is calling the fight off unless he retracts the announcement. "This is going to cost you your title shot and the way you're going you might never get another one."

"I ain't denying it because it's true," says Cassius, "and if you want to call the fight off that's your business. My religion's more important to me than the fight."

We don't have the same problem with the closed circuit around the country as MacDonald does with the live show in Miami Beach. Nationally the controversy seems to be helping rather than hurting the advance ticket sale, but MacDonald is the key. If he doesn't stage the fight on February 25th, we'll have nothing to show.

At the Fifth Street gym Angelo Dundee tells me, "Looks like the fight's off. The Kid just went home to pack."

I run over to MacDonald's office and he's sitting with Chris Dundee, Angelo's brother. "What's this about the fight being called off?" I ask.

"It's off," says MacDonald. "I gave the Kid his choice and he wouldn't go along so I have to call the fight off."

Now I'm thinking about all those tickets we're selling around the country for the closed circuit. "You can't do that," I tell him.

"The hell I can't," he says. "You're a Northerner. You don't understand. You don't realize that Miami is the Deep South and is just as segregated as any town in Mississippi. How can I promote a fight down here with a guy who thinks we're White Devils?"

"You know what you're doing, Bill?" I say. "In this country we have freedom of religion."

"Bullshit," says MacDonald, "and don't you go start hitting me with the Constitution." I can see MacDonald is really unhappy about this whole thing. He is a former doorman who became a millionaire and he wants everybody to love him.

"Bill," I say, "you don't realize what you're doing. You'll go down in history as a promoter who denied a man the right to fight for the title because of his religion." I think this line hooks him. He starts copping a plea. "Jesus, what the hell do you want me to do? It's that Malcolm X. He's responsible for all this trouble and he's practically running the Kid's fight camp. That don't look good."

"Suppose Malcolm X got out of town right away?" I ask. "Would that change your mind?"

He thinks for a minute. "Yeah, maybe things wouldn't look so bad, but how do you get him out? You know how hard-nosed those guys are."

"Let me try," I say. I drive out to the house and Malcolm is sitting on the porch. I tell him it's important I talk to him alone. He gives the Brothers the eye and they fade. "The fight's off," I say.

"Yeah, looks that way."

"Don't have to be," I tell him. "You have to understand MacDonald's position. He's getting a lot of heat. He's agreed to go on with the fight if you get out of town. As things stand right now your man has lost his title shot to say nothing of a lot of money. You can save it." Malcolm thinks for a minute. "I get the message," he says.

"Good." I stick my hand out to shake but Muslims weren't shaking white hands. He touches my wrist with his finger.

Malcolm leaves town that night, but before he leaves he must have de-horned me because next time I see Ali he is more his old warm self and I manage to get him alone. "Do you really think we're all White Devils?" I ask him.

"I ain't sure about you because you ain't blue-eyed, but the real whites were created by a bad black scientist. Before that the whole world was black." Now his great eyes look bigger than ever and he seems awed over what he's telling me. "Didn't you know that Jesus Christ was black? The Space Men are black and our Mother Ship is circulating the Earth all the time. They watching all of you."

Muffo, I just saw a flash in the sky. They could be watching. I'm not saying another word.

Regards,

Harold

Stockholm

STOCKHOLM
JULY 1, 1964

Dear Muffo:

As you know, we're doing the Floyd Patterson-Eddie Machen fight here July 5th, and the Swedes are all excited. They love Patterson here. When Ingemar Johansson wins the title from Patterson in '59 the Swedes are so proud he could have run for king and made it, but Ingemar is a close guy with a kroner and he flies home, packs his bags and announces he is moving to Zurich to become a Swiss citizen. He says the taxes are too high in Sweden.

The Swedes are crushed when their one-and-only world's heavyweight champion runs out on them. The following year Patterson regains the title from Johansson and flies immediately to Sweden where he tells the people to forget Johansson, that he will be their champion. He becomes their idol. Patterson is crazy about Sweden and I understand why when I see those shapely, long-legged Svenska blondes with that warm, understanding look.

So now you got the picture here the day before the fight, which doesn't figure to be much. Machen is on the way down but fast, since he also meets some of those blondes and, while they are more fun than sparring partners, they take more out of you.

There is a rumor that Frank Sinatra is flying in from the States in a chartered plane with a load of friends to be with his buddy Al Silvani, who trains Machen. I discount the story when I hear that Joe E. Lewis, the great night club comedian, whose life he portrayed in the movies, is also on the plane.

Joe E., a dear friend and a brother Friar, rarely wanders from within walking distance of Toots Shor's, and I figure they have to hijack him to get him on a plane to Stockholm. The day after the rumor I check it out and sure enough, Sinatra's plane has landed that morning; and I get it from Marty Gable, the actor, who was on board, that Sinatra and Joe E. have a duel over the Atlantic. The weapons are Jack Daniel's vs. Grant's Twelve Year Old (Lewis is a Scotch drinker). They have to help the combatants to the Grand Hotel and put them to bed.

Late that afternoon I call the Grand and ask for Joe E. After a long wait he finally gets on the phone and here's the way the conversation goes:

"Hy'a Joe, is that really you?"

"It ain't Swifty Morgan." His voice has the sound of a bag of gravel being hauled over cobblestones. "Who's this?"

"It's Harold. What's going on?"

"Don't ask me. I'm still in the kip. What time is it?"

"It's five o'clock."

"Tell you what. I'm gonna shave and shower and I'll walk over to Toots. Meet me there at six and we'll have a drink."

"What the hell are you talking about Toots? You're in Stockholm."

There is a long pause and I know he is looking around the

room and out the window. "Stockholm!! How the hell did I get here?"

Joe comes down about an hour later and we head straight for the bar. I introduce him to Ed Ahlquist, the local promoter, a large, glum man who is wearing one of those shiny, multicolored plaid sports jackets. Joe looks closely at the sports jacket and says, "Somewhere in Brooklyn there is a Chevrolet with the seat covers missing." The line doesn't even get a snicker.

Joe says, "This ain't my town. I'm getting the hell out of here and how did I get here in the first place?" He never remembers getting on the plane or crossing the Atlantic.

Joe is naked without a drink in his hand even on a night-club floor. He protests that he is not an alcoholic because he doesn't drink during the day, but he rarely gets up before five in the afternoon. He is also an incurable gambler at the tables and the race tracks and makes much of his misfortune with Lady Luck in his routines, but he is not the sucker people think he is.

One time he finishes up an engagement at the El Rancho in Vegas and the next day, just before he leaves for the airport, he decides to take one last fling at the dice table and runs a shoot up to $22,000. He has to make a plane connection, but he refuses to pull his money off while the dice are hot so he tells Beldon Kettleman, the Rancho owner, to let his money ride and watch it; then he dashes for the airport.

He forgets about the money until Kettleman tells him, weeks later, that he won $30,000 and that he invested it for him in a piece of property next to the El Rancho. A couple of years later Kettleman sells the property to Howard Hughes and Joe E.'s end is $240,000.

But money means nothing to Lewis and he is the softest

touch in show business. When he walks down Sixth Avenue he hands out five-dollar bills to the drunken panhandlers. "Now don't go and waste this on food," he tells them.

Another time at El Rancho the place becomes infested with water bugs and Joe can't stand the large insects. He goes around clubbing them with his bedroom slipper. He comes home drunk but happy one night. He wins $12,000 and hides the roll. The next day he recalls he won some money but he can't remember where he hides it.

Joe tells the story this way: "I search the god-damn room from top to bottom and I can't find my stash. Now I'm laying in bed trying to figure it out when I see this big bug racing across the carpet. I get down on the floor, grab my bedroom slipper and chase after him on my knees and he's gaining on me. He heads for the bathroom and now I'm gaining on him. He ducks behind the toilet bowl and I just raise my slipper to clobber him when I spy my bankroll and the bug is standing there like he's pointing at it. I had to let him live."

To get back to the fight, it wasn't much. Patterson wins an easy twelve-round decision. Everybody makes the fight except Sinatra. He stays in the bed from the moment he arrives until they all leave for Paris the morning after the fight, but it is a delight to have Joe E. on the scene.

Regards,

Harold

Floyd Patterson

Dear Muffo:

Just get back from Stockholm where Floyd Patterson is just as popular as he was when we do the Patterson-Machen fight four years ago. Although his fight with Jimmy Ellis is a week old, I find guys in bars all over town still arguing about the decision. I see you are amongst them. I get your note saying you think the fight should have been called a draw.

The Swedes, who love Patterson, make a lot of noise every time Patterson throws a punch and although it is a very close fight Howard Cosell is already calling Floyd the winner by the fourteenth round. When Ellis gets the decision there's a lot of loud wailing, to say nothing of Cosell's hysterics.

Personally I think Ellis wins it, although I concede it's very close. But I'm a reasonable man and I figure maybe I'm a little off so I poll the newspapermen and they're all top-notch fight writers, guys like Barney Nagler, British experts like Peter Wilson, the A.P., the U.P.I., Anthony Lewis, *The New York Times* London correspondent who is not a fight writer but is a keen ring observer. All of them think Ellis wins a close fight.

The only guy I find who thinks Patterson wins the fight is

177

Milt Gross of the *Post,* who is Floyd's ghost writer and he tells me he is keeping score for Cosell.

I know Cosell for six years or more, and each year I watch him grow bigger in a business that is as fickle as a nympho at an orgy. I admire and respect Howard for qualities that don't necessarily show up in the ratings. He is a decent man. But I don't regard him as the final word. Last night we rerun the tape of the fight and shut off the sound. With no Cosell and no crowd noises, I'm satisfied it is a fair decision.

This promotion has been a ball-breaker from the go. When Ellis wins the elimination tournament and becomes the WBA champion during Ali's exile, Patterson is looking for a shot to regain the title for the third time. Sweden wants this match badly because of his popularity there, so Mike Malitz and I put the match together and co-promote it with the Swedes.

After three trips to Stockholm we finally get all the pieces together and I call Patterson, tell him everything's set to come in, and sign the contracts. The date of the fight is August 15th. He mumbles something about having to go to the Coast for a few days and he'll sign when he comes back.

While Patterson is out there I hear that he has signed to do a television show to be shot in July. Knowing how long Floyd likes to take to train for a fight I can see there's no way he'll be able to fight in August.

When he comes back he says the fight will have to be postponed until September because he is doing this television show. I ask him how he can put a TV show before a title fight he was so hot for and he says, "I'm not going to be fighting forever. I'm going to become a movie star. If Jim Brown can do it, I can do it."

The Swedes are very unhappy about this news. It's an

outdoor show and there's a big difference there in the weather between August and September. Besides, they are already booking tours and package deals for the fight. They reluctantly agree to a September date, but I ask them to hold off for a couple of days. Maybe I can still fix it.

The TV show is a series called *Wild West,* the one with the two secret service men living out of a railway car and the star and producer is Robert Conrad, no relation. I know that Conrad is a devout boxing nut, so I call him and explain the situation.

"You mean to say this guy is going to postpone a heavyweight title fight to do my show?" he says. "That's crazy. Let me talk to Patterson and I'll try to reschedule the shooting. It's no big deal. He's only getting $1,500."

When I get back to Conrad he says, "I'm sorry, I tried but it's no soap. Patterson is all primed to do his acting in July and doesn't want me to change the schedule."

Now the fight's set for September and the first thing on the agenda is the referee. The fighters insist on an American referee, one they both agree on. There will be no judges.

I make up a list of five referees and call Angelo Dundee, Ellis's manager. The first name he eliminates is Harold Valan. "Valan is a New York State referee," says Angelo. "That might be an edge for Patterson. I don't want him, but give me a few days to go over the list."

When I call Patterson and read him the referee list I tell him Dundee doesn't want Valan. "Then I want him," he says. When I remind Patterson about this conversation he says he doesn't even remember me calling him. After much bickering with Dundee, he finally concedes and agrees to go along with Valan.

The day before the fight we have a rules meeting for the

press and the fighters. Valan, who is laying down the rules, is sitting between Ellis and Patterson. If you see the Johnny Carson show the other night you must hear Patterson say he never hears of Valan or sees him until he climbs into the ring the night of the fight. I don't believe my ears. Patterson is screaming in his dressing room after the fight that he was jobbed and blames it all on the referee. He makes no bones about it and says that Valan is in the pay of the Dundees. He also says that Valan is hanging out with the Dundees and living at their hotel—which is not true. He is living at my hotel and we once accidentally run into Angelo when he's having dinner.

Patterson has made some serious accusations so I call a press conference for later in the evening so he can get everything off his chest. The press shows up, but Floyd doesn't. Where is he? Cosell's going to the airport and he's helping him with his bags.

Regards,

Harold

Marianne Moore

NEW YORK
SEPTEMBER 12, 1970

Dear Muffo:

George Plimpton is an old buddy of mine and for a couple of years he's after me to do him a special favor. His big ambition is to put Marianne Moore, the poet, together with Muhammad Ali, the poet. Every time I try to arrange it there's a conflict in Muhammad's schedule.

I once meet Marianne Moore and somebody tells her I do most of Muhammad's fights. I know she's a sports nut and has written poems about Hodges and the baseball Mets. But she's had more than twelve works published and a lot of her stuff is witty, intellectual and often satirical. She's eighty years old and has a collection published this year. Now you got to take your hat off to anybody that's eighty years old and still going to the plate. She's also a Pulitzer Prize winner.

When you sit with her you're oblivious to her age. She's agile and curious and her lively eyes are like two shiny buttons. Back on her head she wears a black three-cornered hat that looks like she might have got it at the same sale Paul Revere got his.

She tells me she is a big fan of Muhammad's and she's

impatiently looking forward to meeting him. Ali is in town for two days and I finally nail him down. He don't know Marianne Moore from Grace Moore and I explain who she is. He asks me if she read any of his poetry. I say, "I'm afraid so," but the crack goes over his head. He thinks he's Walt Whitman. He's leaving for Chicago late the next afternoon so I call Plimpton and tell him. He's all excited. "We'll have tea at Toots Shor's," he says.

The next day I pick Ali up and we go over to Toots's. George and Marianne are seated in a corner at a head table. Muhammad slithers in next to the little old lady and she immediately starts talking about fights and about his poetry. Plimpton is beaming. She's ecstatic.

Al Buck, the late veteran boxing writer for *The Post* and an old friend of Ali's, sees us and sits down at the table. Plimpton growls at him and shoos him away. "This is my exclusive," he says.

After a while Plimpton says, "I have a great idea. Why don't you two poets write a poem? One write a line, then the other write a line, and keep alternating." "That's a marvelous idea," says Marianne. Ali agrees, thinking now he's trapped without his rhyme book.

Now we look for some paper and there's none handy, so George smooths out his napkin and says, "Let's do it on this."

While they're doodling I go over to have a drink with Al Buck and unruffle his feelings. After about a half hour I go back to the table and they seem to be through with the masterpiece. Then Ali says he has to run to catch a plane and he leaves.

About ten minutes later I get up to go. I'm at the check

room when Plimpton comes running out and he's all shook up. "Where's the napkin?" he yells. "How the hell do I know?" I answer. "You had it on the table." I've always known Plimpton as a calm, unflappable guy but now he's getting irksome and he's inferring that I stole the god-damn napkin.

We go back to the table and it turns out that when the waiter clears off the table he takes the linen and now the napkin is somewhere in the kitchen. We go to the kitchen and they tell us that all the soiled linen gets thrown down the laundry chute. Plimpton's frantic. I leave him in the kitchen and go back and sit with Marianne. She is not at all perturbed. About ten minutes later George comes out the kitchen, sweaty and breathless. He is holding up the napkin.

Lovingly he smooths it out on the table and I read it. I think maybe it's the worst thing I ever read, but Marianne is happy and that's what it's all about.

After we defeat Ernie Terrell,
He will get nothing, nothing but Hell
Terrell was big, ugly and tall,
But when he fights me he is sure to fall.
If he criticizes this poem and me and
    Miss Moore,
To prove he is not the champ she will
    stop him in four.
He is claiming to be the real
    heavyweight champ,
But when the fight starts he will look
    like a tramp.

He has been talking too much about me
   and making me sore.
After I'm through with him he will
   not be able to challenge Miss Moore.

Regards,

Harold

Sonny Liston, I

Dear Muffo:

Here for two days to see some old friends and shoot a little craps. Took Sonny Liston and his wife, Geraldine, to dinner last night. He's got some kind of action going here, but it's got nothing to do with the fight business.

After the show at the Dunes we go to the Flamingo Lounge and Sonny knocks off a half-dozen quick double Scotch-and-sodas. He's in a great mood.

About ten years ago I win a bet from him and he owes me six custom-made shirts, but he never pays off. For years, every time I see him I say, "Where's the shirts, Sonny?" He always says, "One of these days you're gonna get 'em." I finally quit bringing it up.

Last night, out of nowhere he says, "Listen, ya' New York bum, you're gonna get them shirts."

"At last," I say. "When am I gonna get them?"

"When ah owns a shirt factory," he says. He slams the table with his fist and you can hear him laughing all over the joint.

Then Geraldine says, "What's the matter with Joe Louis? I hear he's been sick."

"Don't you know, Sonny?" I ask.

"If she'd a'know, I'd a'know," he says. "What's a'matter with him?"

So I tell him how some dame got Joe hooked on H and that he was mainlining it, but now he's taking the cure and while it was real tough on him, he was beating it.

Sonny's got the world's most ferocious scowl and now he's giving it to me and his Svengali eyes start blazing.

"You son of a bitch," he says. "You say that about my man. He wouldn't do a dumb thing like that."

"It's not exactly a secret," I tell him. "It's been printed in a couple of places." This wouldn't have made much difference to Sonny because he can't read anyway.

"Them mother fuckers'll print anything," he says. "You say that about Joe Louis. He's been my idol since I been a kid."

He goes on raving and Geraldine tries to quiet him down. I can see the evening is over so I call for the check.

The next day I get a phone call at the hotel. It's Sonny. "Hello ya' New York bum," he says. I say "Hello," and there's two minutes of silence, but I can hear him breathing. Finally he says, "I just found out. You wuz right about Joe. I wanna apologize."

How about that, Sonny Liston apologizing. I think it's the first time in his life he ever copped a plea.

If I go back to New York via Chicago, I'll call you from the airport.

Best,

Harold

Sonny Liston, II

Dear Muffo:

It's old news now that Sonny Liston's dead. The Las Vegas Coroner's Office announced that he died of an overdose of heroin. Bullshit, Sonny didn't just die. He was murdered. Homicides aren't supposed to happen in Las Vegas. Bad for the town's image, you know. Sure, Sonny died of an O-D, but somebody else pumped him with the stuff.

It happened on December 30th, 1970. His wife, Geraldine, who had been out of town, found his body when she came home on January 5th, 1971. The Sheriff's Office found the puncture marks all right and neatly wrapped up the case. If there was any further investigation, the public never heard about it. What pisses me off is that nobody seems to care, but I'll bet my life he was murdered and I'll tell you why.

Sonny was scared to death of needles. I remember when he is training in Boston and he is coming down with the flu. The doc is going to give him a shot of B-12 and when Sonny gets a flash at that needle he wants to throw the doc out the window. And I told you how he reacts when he finds out about Joe Louis.

Another thing, Sonny is a heavy boozer. He loves to drink and heroin isn't a boozer's bag. He smokes a little pot and does a little snorting once in a while, but he never goes for hard drugs, and I know him pretty well.

I put a lot of time in Vegas doing three big fights there and I got to meet all kinds of characters so I start to do a little checking and the pieces begin to fall in place.

First you gotta understand that Sonny had a prison mentality after all that time in the can. Now he's living in Vegas, retired from the ring. He's got some dough stashed, but not much and he's looking for action. Some very tough citizens are running a loan-shark factory and doing some pushing out of East Las Vegas and since Sonny used to be a head-knocker for unions around St. Louis, they figure he makes an impressive associate and they hire him.

It's good casting. If I don't know Sonny and he comes after me to collect, I pay up quick because he scares the shit out of you just looking at you. But he's not satisfied just being a collector. He wants a bigger piece of the action.

Meantime, Sonny is getting drunk around town, making scenes and putting pressure on these guys. Being the former heavyweight champion of the world don't cut any ice with the shylocks or pushers. They're not about to let anybody cut in on their turf.

One night they take him out on a party. After he gets stinking drunk they take him home, jab him with an O-D, and that's the end of Sonny.

I talked off the record to a guy in the Sheriff's Office and here's what he said: "A bad nigger. He got what was coming to him."

I don't buy that. He had some good qualities. He had a

great dignity about him. He reminded me of some fierce African tribal chief; and those sports writers gave him plenty of respect in his presence. Some day they might do a movie of his life. Make a hell of a picture.

A year before Liston fought Patterson for the title, Irving Kahn, who is the head of Telepromoter, calls me in one day and says, "Sonny Liston is the No. 1 contender for the title and probably the next heavyweight champion, but he's a hot potato. You got to do a job on him. You got to paint those prison stripes off him." That's how I got involved with Sonny.

Liston was born in Arkansas in 1932. I think he died the day he was born. He was his father's 25th kid with two wives. Got his first pair of shoes when he was nine, never went to school and ran away from home when he was thirteen. By the time he is sixteen he is a two-hundred-pounder and strong enough to lift the front end of a Ford with his bare hands.

He's the leader of a tough gang of kids around East St. Louis and winds up with a rap sheet long enough to paper your bathroom wall. He's picked up by the St. Louis police more than a hundred times, arrested nineteen and convicted twice.

When he's eighteen he gets two-and-a-half to five for holding up a gas station and is shipped to the Missouri State pen, where they keep some of the toughest cons in the country. Thurlo Baker, one of the arresting officers, tells me the best thing ever happened to Liston was going to the pen, where he learned how to box. "If he hadn't become a boxer," he says, "he'd probably be dead with a bullet in his back."

The Jefferson City Prison housed three thousand men,

two thirds white and one third black. The white cons are divided up into governing cliques. A guy named Hank Colouris headed up the West Siders, Nick Baroudi heads up the Italian gang, and a guy named Frankie leads a bunch called the East Siders and they're always pushing blacks around.

One day Baroudi leads his bunch against a few blacks and lays them out. Liston is in the yard when it starts and he makes straight for Baroudi and hits him a shot in the jaw. "Every time you touch a colored boy you gonna get a taste of that," he tells him, "and that goes for those other two punk ofays. If ya'all don't like it you can meet me in the storage room."

Now I know this sounds like a Jimmy Cagney movie but it's a matter of record. The three gang leaders show up in the storage room to cut Sonny down to size and the betting is he don't come out alive. Ten minutes later he walks out alone. The three bad guys are stretched out on the floor.

Father Stevens, who is the Pat O'Brien of the joint, tells Sonny this kind of violence can only get his sentence extended. The good father with an eye for boxing talent convinces him to go out for the boxing team, but the betting in the Yard is that he hasn't got long to live.

"We really thought his number was up," Sam Lincoln, an ex-con who did time with Liston, tells me. "White guys never got away with that kind of shit and you know for sure they ain't gonna take it from a black guy, but I think Father Stevens makes some moves."

Anyhow, nothing happens to Sonny and once he starts boxing in the prison tournaments they all become his fans. He gets paroled in '52, gets a job, gets married and mops up the Golden Gloves in '53. Then he turns pro and knocks out everybody in sight.

He wins fourteen of his first fifteen bouts, losing one to Marshall, who clips Sonny when he's laughing and breaks his jaw. But he beats Marshall in the return match in '56, then is out of action until '58 and for good reason. He is arrested for slugging a cop.

This is the worst move Sonny ever makes because slugging a cop is like spitting on the flag and every cop in every town who hears about it makes a mental note.

Sonny said the cop was drunk. The cop was writing out a traffic ticket for Liston's cab driver. Sonny says he made a few cracks and the cop says, "You one of them smart niggers," and starts taking out his gun. "I just took the gun away from him." He never did explain how the cop wound up with a seven-stitch gash over his eye.

Liston gets nine months in the workhouse, which is an easy rap and burns up the cops. But by now Sonny has a mob guy with connections managing him.

Sonny's number is up in every precinct in St. Louis. While he is out on bail he is arrested four times and released each time. It's no secret on the force that if the right spot comes up, Sonny could get his brains blown out.

His managers decided St. Louis is getting too hot and they move him to Philadelphia, the City of Brotherly Love. He gets in trouble trying to pick up a dame in the park in the middle of the night and the whole story is blown out of proportion.

On a trip to Denver, Sonny meets a priest named Father Edward Murphy, a kindly, patient man who feels that Sonny has been given a bad deal by society. After the Phily's mess-up Sonny decides to become a Catholic and goes to Denver to repent, but he doesn't pursue the call for long. Since he can't read, learning the catechism gets a little tough and he quits in boredom.

Back in Philly the cops are still giving him a hard time so he moves to Denver. Now he's heavyweight champion of the world and he's really on his good behavior. I don't want to make this sound like hearts and flowers, but he really loves kids and always has a flock of 'em around the house. His wife can't have any.

But in Denver it's the same thing with the cops. They keep harassing him. When he drives around, they tail him in a squad car, waiting for him to make a mistake.

After a couple of years he gives up Denver and moves to Las Vegas and you know the rest of the story. Somehow I get the feeling that this was all written down someplace the day he was born in that broken-down hovel in Arkansas almost fifty years ago.

Sonny was a hell of a fighter at one time, maybe one of the best, but I guess you can't win 'em all.

Keep punching,

Harold

Butty Sugrue

Dear Muffo:

When I check into the hotel here yesterday there are three messages waiting for me to call a guy named Butty Sugrue. I call the number and this guy's telling me he met with Joe Louis last year. I think I'm talking to Barry Fitzgerald. His brogue's got a brogue and I can barely make out what the hell he's saying.

Finally it gets through to me that he is telling me he is going to make me rich and is insisting that I meet him at his pub at my earliest convenience. I figure that anybody who is going to make me rich is worth a little time so I hop a cab over to Shepherd's Bush where his pub, The Wellington, is located. This may be the largest beer joint in London and it's all Irish. It's run by Sugrue, his wife and all their relatives and it looks like the staging area for the I.R.A.

Butty used to be a strongman by trade. He once pulls a double-decker bus across the O'Connel Bridge in Dublin with a tow rope in his teeth. His gimmicks are well known in Ireland. He was the resident strongman with Duffy's Circus, he's promoted some fights and he once has himself buried in the ground for over thirty days.

Sugrue is about five-foot-eight and built like a mini-tank with a chest like a round house and a neck like a Brahma bull. This talking Blarney Stone says to me, "Could you get Muhammad Ali for a fight in Dublin?"

"Against whom?" I counter.

"I leave that up to you," he says.

I tell him it could be arranged if the money was right. He sticks his pudgy meat hook at me and says, "We got a deal, let's shake."

Every town I go into has a guy who wants to promote a Muhammad Ali fight and he always has the money until it's time to put it up. I tell him it's nowhere near a deal until he can convince me he can come up with the bread.

"No problem a'tall, not a'tall," he says. "How much will it take?"

Ali is getting a quarter of a million for those fights since he hasn't got the title. I give Sugrue a ballpark figure of $300,000 to get the promotion off the ground.

"That's nothing a'tall, not a'tall," he says. "Come with me." He walks me around the corner to his bank and into the bank president's office. It's the William Glynn Bank. "Mr. Moriarty," says Sugrue, "would you tell this mon I'm good for three hundred thousand dollars."

Mr. Moriarity gives me that banker's fish-eye look and says, "Yes, Butty Sugrue is good for $300,000. This bank stands behind him."

"And there's more where that comes from," says Butty.

I lay out the ground rules for him. If I can put a match together he will have to put up a letter of credit for the fighters' purses. He will pay all expenses and we will share the profits, fifty-fifty. I make it clear that I am not putting up one dime.

He agrees. "You'll be thanking the day you met me," he says. "We'll sell out every seat we put up in Dublin."

I'm flying back to the States in a few days and I'll let you know what happens.

Regards,

Harold

Dublin, I

Dear Muffo:

Didn't get a chance to write from New York, I've been so busy, but the Dublin match is made and I'm here looking the place over.

Don Elbaum has a heavyweight named Al "Blue" Lewis who nobody wants to fight. He's a big, strong bruiser with 19 knockouts in 34 starts and he's ranked, but he spends some of his best years in the slammer like Liston. Elbaum wants $50,000 for Lewis. I offer him $25,000, take it or leave it. He takes it.

I talk to Herbert, Ali's manager, and the asking price is a quarter of a million. I tell Herbert how poor the people are in Ireland and remind him he owes me money because I got screwed on the deal when Ali fights a guy named Blinn in Zurich last year. He finally agrees to go for two hundred thousand.

With the fighters getting two hundred and twenty-five thousand, that leaves me with a seventy-five-thousand-dollar cushion to run the promotion, which shouldn't be too tough at Dublin's prices. There's only one problem. Nobody here believes there is going to be an Ali fight.

I tell them the contracts are signed and the letters of credit are up, but nobody's buying it. They make jokes about it in the newspapers. This is the hard way to get people excited about a fight that's going to have to draw $300,000 to break even.

I ask Tom Mylar, one of the local sports writers, why everybody is so skeptical. "It's Butty Sugrue," he says. "He don't go for spit. Nobody believes he's coming up with $300,000. He runs out on a fight promotion a couple of years ago and all Ireland is wise to his gimmicks. He'll do anything for publicity."

"But the money is up," I tell him, "and we've put a deposit on Croke Park for a July 19th date."

"He'll find some excuse to take the money down after he gets all the publicity he wants," says Mylar.

I can't convince anybody that Sugrue is legally bound by contract for the money and Sugrue is laying a lot of Irish curses on the disbelievers.

I'm not going to worry about it. I got two months before I get the promotion rolling full steam, but something tells me these Irishmen are not going to believe there is going to be an Ali fight until he puts both feet on the Old Sod.

Regards,

Harold

Dick and Dutch

NEW YORK
JUNE 10, 1972

Dear Muffo:

While you're in Europe the damndest thing happens here. Nixon appoints a commission, headed by ex-Governor Schaeffer of Pennsylvania, to investigate the use and effects of drugs. When Schaeffer reports the results he tells Nixon they find that marijuana is harmless or at least less harmful than tobacco or booze. Nixon says, "I refuse to accept that," and pours more of our dough into Mexico to cut off pot.

There's got to be ten million pot smokers in America and in another couple of years there'll probably be twenty million. If you want to get down to it clinically, alcohol is a drug and a harmful one. It can kill you. We know enough of our newspaper friends who went down the tube as a direct result. I never hear of anybody dying from smoking pot. But Nixon drinks Scotch and it's more than a rumor that he gets bombed out every once in a while. So did LBJ drink and Jack Kennedy and Harry Truman and F.D.R.

It's hard to convince kids today that drinking booze was once against the law. I had my first drink in a speakeasy. Remember—you knock on the door, a guy looks through the peep hole and he lets you in if he knows you. And even if he don't know you he lets you in if you don't look like a fink. Getting busted was a joke.

I never forget that first time in a speakeasy. Maybe it's exciting because you're breaking the law but the whole thing seems crazy. I look around the bar and I see judges, lawyers, detectives, newspapermen and everybody's breaking the law. Now the same thing is happening with marijuana; but if they catch you in most states they can put you in the slammer for a longer stretch than if you held up a bank.

While I don't think a guy who smokes a joint is any more a criminal than a guy who drinks a martini, I don't believe marijuana should be legalized, but it certainly should be decriminalized. Pot is strictly a recreational weed and takes some sophistication to handle. The problem lies in the indiscretion of the users.

I don't know how much of a dent alcoholism puts in the productivity of this country, but I feel that legalizing pot would decrease our production a hell of a lot more.

My beef lies with the idiotic propaganda and outright lies the government has disseminated about the effects of pot down through the years. Instead of presenting an intelligent issue on the danger of marijuana, it has fractured its credibility by trying to scare the shit out of everybody with a lot of nonsense, and that's a more serious problem than the pot itself.

Once you lie to the kids, they're not going to believe anything else you tell them and they go on to experimenting with insidious drugs like heroin. I don't think young kids should smoke pot. They shouldn't drink booze, either, or mug old ladies. That's up to the kid's old man, not the government, to control.

What I resent is the politically motivated laboratory tests that tell you one stick of marijuana is more harmful to the lungs than fourteen Chesterfields, or that it induces rape, robbery, and homicide, or throwing it into the same bag with heinous drugs. A perfect example is Nixon's rejection of the Schaeffer report. That's all a joke to pot smokers.

I'm sure that clinically you could find many negatives in marijuana, but you could do the same thing with a hundred foods and beverages we consume every day. On the other hand, pot has its therapeutic values in this world of tension and I certainly would prescribe it over Valium or the dozens of other legal addictive pills millions are popping every day.

Granted smoking pot is an indiscretion: Man and woman are entitled to a few indiscretions as long as they aren't bothering anybody else.

It must be over thirty-five years ago that I smoked my first joint. Got turned on by a guy named Dickie Wells, a man-about-town up in Harlem who ran some night clubs. He was a light-skinned, good-looking cat and sharp as a double-edged razor.

It was pretty rough on the blacks in those days. There weren't many places they were allowed to go, but that didn't bother Dickie. He use to put on a turban and go on cruises "passing" as an Indian swami who vowed never to speak his mother tongue while he was in this hemisphere. He did great with the broads.

He calls me one night and says, "I'm going to pick you up and take you over to hear Louis Satchmo Armstrong on

Fifty-Second Street." When he comes over he tells me Satchmo is out of reefer and he's bringing him some. At this time I'm very vague about reefer. I never hear it called pot. He claims Armstrong says it is medicine and is good for headaches, toothaches and the blues.

Marijuana had just become a dirty word around this time. Some martinet named Anslinger who is the Federal Narcotics Chief is putting out all kinds of ridiculous propaganda about it and classifies it as a dangerous drug. Meantime LaGuardia starts his own New York City investigation of marijuana and his commission comes up with the same report that the Schaeffer Commission did, which Nixon rejects years later. But the government suppresses it so now I know which is the true one.

Dickie Wells lights up a joint and I smoke half of it with him; then we go to the club to hear Louis. Now Armstrong blows a pretty good horn, but this night he sounds like Gabriel. Everything is mellow. The people look beautiful, the music is great and my taste buds are never so sensitive.

I tell myself this could be a boon to civilization—not aware that it has been a boon to several civilizations for several thousand years.

The other night I'm thinking about Nixon's pot phobia and this fantasy comes to me. In it, two joints alter the history of the Vietnam War. It goes like this:

It's the early part of '69. Nixon has had his dinner and he is in the Oval Office going over some papers. He has a meeting with Kissinger in a half-hour.

A mess boy enters carrying a tray with some glasses, ice and a bottle of Scotch. As he puts it on the table he doesn't see a folded Kleenex drop out of his white mess jacket. A few minutes later Nixon gets up to mix a drink. He sees the Kleenex, picks it up and two thinly rolled cigarettes drop out. He picks up the joints, examines them, smells them and says to himself, "That little Filipino bastard, I'll have him court-martialed for this."

Now he takes the joints back to his desk and examines them some more. "So this is what all that shit is about," he says. "Lot of people smoking it. Trying to crap me it's harmless. What if it really is. Maybe I ought to try it. Yeah, think I'll take a shot at it."

He lights up a joint and smokes the whole thing. Now he's sitting rigidly, waiting for something to happen. "This is a god-damned waste of time," he says. Before he knows it he's got his feet up on his desk, he's leaning back in his swivel chair and his hands are clasped behind the back of his neck.

"This is just a god-damned... this is... hey... this is nice ... Oh, boy ... I haven't felt this relaxed since I was a baby." Now the tightness has left his face and even his jowls are happy.

A few minutes later there's a knock at the door. It's Kissinger. "Hy'a Dutch. Come on in. Grab a chair and sit down," says Nixon.

"My, but you look comfortable, Mizzder Prezident."

"Henry, I've never felt more comfortable in my life."

"I have good news for you, Mizzder Prezident. I have been at the Pentagon all day and they have finalized da logistics for your plan to bomb Cambodia."

"My plan to bomb Cambodia? You mean that was my idea?"

"Are you sure you're feeling all right, Mizzder Prezident?"

"You're just not with it, Henry. I'm feeling great." Nixon

gets up and tunes in some jazz on the hi-fi and turns it loud. He don't want the tapes to pick up any of this dialogue. "Dig that sound, Dutch, isn't that a wild bass?"

"Are you sure you're all right, Mizzder Prezident?"

"God damn it, I told you I was fine. I don't think I'm getting through to you." Nixon reaches into his drawer, takes out the other joint and hands it to Kissinger. "Here, smoke this, that's a presidential order, and keep your voice low."

"But this is marijuana, Mizzder Prezident."

"Just smoke it."

Kissinger lights up and starts puffing away. "Shouldn't vee be getting back to the war, Mizzder Prezident?"

"War? What war? Oh, the war. Henry, I've just decided not to bomb Cambodia. That would be a terrible thing to do. We'd be killing a lot of gentle, innocent people, driving them out of their homes and off their farms. After all those gooks . . . I mean those people are really our brothers under the skin. All this killing has got to stop."

"But Mizzder Prezident, you said we had to neutralize the supply lines . . . you said so what if we kill a lot of Vietnamese and Cambodians, they all look alike anyway."

"Wasn't that an awful thing to say?"

"Ve're losing dis war, Mizzder Prezident, and that schmuck Westmoreland gives me alibis, nothing but alibis . . . nothing but . . . but . . . Hello dere . . . Hoo-ha . . . Oh, boy . . . Suddenly, Mizzder Prezident, I'm feeling like the whole Luftwaffe . . . I'm floating . . . I'm soaring . . ."

"It's really something, isn't it, Henry?"

"Some of dem Hollywood starlets I date smoke dis stuff. Dey say it's good for zex?"

"See, you don't know who to believe these days. My experts say it's bad for sex."

"Different strokes for different folks, Dickie-Boy."

"This stuff sure makes you hungry. I got the munchies. Think I'll send Jerry out for some Mars bars and some Twinkies, How about you, Dutch?"

"I'm drooling, Dickie-Boy. Right now I would trade in Prince Sihanouk for a *sacher torte*."

"I thought you already traded him in."

"Oh, dot's right. How about Lon Nol for a Tootsie Roll?"

Muffo, this is where my fantasy ends. Now, if you can figure out a way to get Nixon turned on . . .

Sincerely,

Harold

Dublin, II

Dear Muffo:

The Ali-"Blue" Lewis fight is only two days away, and I got problems. Sugrue is trying to run the promotion like a pop-and-mom grocery store. Handling the tickets for a big stadium like Croke Park is a professional job, but Butty insists that his wife and a trusted friend handle the tickets and they haven't the slightest idea what the hell they're doing.

I recommend a professional box office man, but Butty says, "I ain't lettin' no thievin' Mick touch my money." And up until yesterday I couldn't find a twenty-foot ring in all of Ireland. I talked to the top promoter in Belfast and he said he had a twenty-foot ring, but I'd have to send up for it. Problem is the "troubles" are on in full swing in Northern Ireland; if you get your head in the wrong place at the wrong time you could get it blown off.

I finally get a couple of guys to make the run to Belfast and I got to give them double pay. They bring the ring back yesterday and the ground crew starts to assemble it. I see it's only a sixteen-footer and Angelo Dundee will never go for that. Then I find out that the army has a twenty-footer and after a lot of calls I get it delivered this morning.

The ground crew is made up of eight silent Hibernians Butty imports from County Cork, all relatives. This morning I lay out the ring plans for them and tell them the ring must not be any lower than four feet and any higher than four-and-a-half feet off the ground. They all nod and when I go back at noon they got it almost five-and-a-half feet up. They take it down and when I return at four o'clock they got it three-and-a-half feet up.

Ali takes the town by storm. I was right. They don't believe there's a fight until he gets off the plane. Thousands of Irishmen jam the airport and damn near take the joint apart. I got a sleeper up my sleeve. I know that Ali's mother's maiden name is O'Shea, but he don't like to talk about "the slave names them slave owners gave our people." I ask him if he'll mention it and he's so overwhelmed by the crowd that he goes into a big spiel about his mother being an O'Shea, and they go wild.

The biggest fight name around here is Billy Conn. Every Irishman will tell you that Billy had Joe Louis beat going into the thirteenth until he stuck his chin out. I guess he's the best they got and they're very proud of him.

The other day I call Billy in Pittsburgh and tell him I'm sending him a plane ticket and five hundred pocket money, to get his ass over here. He's never been to Ireland. "I'll do it for laughs," he says and grabs the first plane out.

Billy is smashed when he gets off the plane and he stays that way. Here is his routine when he makes the rounds of the pubs: "This is the worst god-damn country I've ever been in. And am I glad my ancestors took the boat out or I'd a' been stuck here." It gets a little embarrassing.

I got Joe Bugner, the European champion, in the semifinal and the other morning I look in and see his manager, Andy Smith, packing. I ask him where he's going and he says, "Getting the hell out of here. We just got a kidnap threat. Some crazy group from up North say they're going to kidnap Joe."

They got nothing against Bugner. They hate Scotchmen and Andy Smith is Scotch. I get him some extra security and quiet him down, but nobody snatches Bugner. I'm disappointed. It would have been a nice touch.

John Huston has been in town all week following the action. He had a few fights when he was a kid and he is a real fan, loves Ali. Ernie Anderson, his press agent, tells me John just screened his new movie, *Fat City*, at the Cannes Film Festival. It's based on the fight novel of the same name.

The picture isn't going to open in the States for a month so I suggest to Ernie that they have a special screening here since we got the fight writers in town from England, Europe and a few from America. Ernie gets a theater and announces it with a big fanfare. Everybody from both fight camps shows up. The movie is beautifully done with all the nuances and all the schtik, in the gym, in the ring, before and after the fight. Halfway through the picture I see Ali dozing off. Blue Lewis is asleep and so is Bundini. These guys do this shit every day and they're not at all entertained by what they're watching. They're cops and robbers guys. Huston thinks it's funny.

I'm trying to find out how much we got in the box office. Butty and his wife aren't sure and they got the money. The ringsides are practically sold out at fifteen pounds a head, that's about forty bucks, but we only got about three thousand of those. We got over fifty thousand seats in the stands and the stands sale is weak.

I tell Butty that if something exciting doesn't happen real fast, it's going to cost him a bundle.

"Don't worry about a t'ing," he tells me. "Didn't you hear what I got the Bishop to say after Mass Sunday? He said the fight was a good cause as the mentally handicapped children were going to get a percentage of the profits. Now the wives won't make no fuss when the husband spends some of the house money on a ticket. They'll be storming the gates on the day of the fight."

Maybe he knew something I didn't know, but that didn't make much sense to me. "Butty," I say, "you better understand this now. The way things are going you won't be giving those poor kids enough money to buy a Tootsie Roll."

"I ain't worried a'tall, not a'tall," he says.

Ali has been going to hospitals and orphan asylums and he's got the whole town's traffic screwed up. Hundreds of people hang around the entrance of the Gresham Hotel just to get a look at him and this gives me a clue. I think once they've seen him they've seen him and they're not buying a ticket to see him fight.

Last night I get further evidence that does not bolster my optimism. I'm in a pub arguing with this big Irishman—you got to argue with these guys or they get mad at you—and I ask him if he bought a ticket to the fight.

"I'm going but I ain't paying," he said. "It's an affront to ask an Irishman to pay to see a fight."

"Did someone give you a ticket?" I ask.

"Nobody gave me a ticket, but I'll be there."

"How you going to get in?" I ask.

"That's for me to know and you to find out," he says, smirking in his ale.

I wish I was in Monte Carlo.

Regards,

Harold

Dublin, III

Dear Muffo:

It's all over now, but I blew it. I should have known that big Hibernian was trying to tell me something when he said it's an affront for an Irishman to pay to see a fight. At least five thousand of them cracked through the outfield fence and infiltrated the stands at Croke Park yesterday. In addition, a lot of the ticket sellers they hire for the night go into business for themselves and are passing in guys for whatever they can get.

I think Butty Sugrue is still working on his abacus to find out how much he loses. All I know is he's going to have to sell a lot of beer in his pub to break even. I think he blows around $140,000. The last time I see him he says, "I'm not worried a'tall, not a'tall." I am because he owes me six grand for transportation expenses.

As you probably know by now, Ali wins it on a technical knockout in the eleventh round though Lewis tries hard all the way and takes a terrible pasting. I've seen worse fights, but the real action comes after it's over.

There's better than twenty-five thousand people in the joint and the minute the referee raises Ali's hand everybody

213

tries to get into the ring. I got Prime Minister Jack Lynch and Bishop Casey sitting together in the third row of the working press and this stampede comes across, sweeping them out of the way, stepping on typewriters and kicking sports writers in the head in this mad dash to get into the ring, which is supposed to be secured by the Gardai. That's what they call the cops here.

When I'm a kid back in Brooklyn, the toughest guy in the neighborhood is the Irish cop on the beat. He doesn't take any shit from anybody. Now I'm in Ireland where they all come from and I figure these guys here can handle the action, but they get knocked on their ass like everybody else and they don't do much about it. They're really intimidated.

The ring is packed with guys punching and shoving and screaming like banshees and Ali is in the middle of all this. It takes fifteen minutes to get him through the mob to his dressing room.

Never had a fight scene quite like this, but it's been laughs and what a cast of characters passes through our suite at the Gresham: priests and playwrights and poets and hookers and I.R.A. gun runners and half the roster of the Abbey Players plus John Huston and Peter O'Toole.

After the fight I have a couple of drinks with the horsey set and one guy says, "Good show, old man, marvelously staged. Superb actor that Ali. He knew exactly when to throw punches and when to pull back. Good actor too, that Lewis fellow."

I look at this guy like he's putting me on, but he isn't. He means it.

"Do you honestly believe this thing was staged?" I ask.

"Obvious, obvious old man," he says. "You know Ali wouldn't be coming to Dublin to have a real fight for this kind of money, but no offense. It was a damn good show."

The guy tells me he is a gentleman jockey and now I got a pretty good idea of the state of horse racing in Ireland.

Almost forget to tell you, I take Ali to the Irish parliament a few days ago to meet the prime minister and Ali spends fifteen minutes telling him how they can settle all the troubles up North although Ali hasn't the slightest idea what they're fighting about, but Prime Minister Lynch just sucks on his pipe and listens.

Ali has a ball here, although this is probably the only country he's been to where there weren't a lot of brothers hanging around. A few days after he arrives he calls me and says, "Hey, man, where are all the niggers in this town?"

Governor Reagan has been in town all week and has the suite down the hall from me. I don't see Nancy around and must assume she's not on the trip, but the governor has Ron Jr. with him—a nice friendly little guy around eleven or twelve.

The kid is crazy about Ali and I ask him if he'd like to see the fight. He'd love to but he has to ask his father. The next day he tells me his father said he can go. When Ali comes over to the hotel I get him to pose for a picture with young Ron and give the kid four tickets to the fight, two for the security men. He's delirious.

Later, Reagan stops me in the lobby to thank me. "He's marvelous, that Ali," he says, giving me the big smile, and I'm looking him right in the eye when he says it. A few years ago, when Ali is in exile and I try to get him a license in

California, the commission is amenable, but Reagan tells them, "I don't want that draft dodger ever to fight in my state."

Sincerely,

Harold

Evel Knievel

Dear Muffo:

I don't know what kind of coverage Evel Knievel's Snake River Canyon jump got in London yesterday, but the coverage in the States for this absurd non-event was fantastic. The lead story on page one of *The New York Times* announced that President Ford had pardoned Nixon. Below it was the story of Knievel's aborted jump.

There were shrill headlines that called it "a hype," but I don't know what the media is complaining about. They're the ones who hyped this thing. We had close to four hundred newsmen, radio and television people, plus one hundred and four still photographers covering the jump and the radio and TV people were prohibited from filming or broadcasting it "live."

When this project was in the talking stages, I vaguely knew Knievel as a motorcycle daredevil. I saw him break his ass on television when he made one of his ill-fated jumps in front of Caesar's Palace. But I couldn't figure out how a guy was going to jump one third of a mile across the canyon on a motorcycle.

Six weeks before the jump was scheduled I flew out here

to consult with the producer, Don Branker, on the layout for the press compound. That's when I got my first look at the do-it-yourself rocket that was going to hurdle the canyon with Evel inside it. The thing looked like a giant beer bottle and the attempt was going to take all guts and very little skill because Knievel would have no control over it except to pull a lever that released a parachute.

As I tried to visualize this thing I got a picture of them sticking a giant firecracker up Knievel's ass and someone lighting the fuse.

Branker was an able young man who had been successful in producing several huge outdoor rock concerts. He had long, flowing blond hair and after Evel first met him he said, "Get rid of that guy. I don't want no goddamned, long-haired hippie around this promotion." That was my first insight to Knievel. But Branker stayed on and it was fortunate that he did.

They tested the rocket while I was there and I watched the big beer bottle shoosh up in a lazy arc and plunk into the swirling green waters of the Snake River below. I said to myself the thing is never going to get to the other side in a thousand years and this crazy bastard is going to kill himself.

I found out later that the same thing had been running through Knievel's mind. When we were drinking, which was every night, Evel would say, in mockery, "I don't want to go, I don't want to go," but he wasn't kidding.

Knievel rode with the devil too many times not to have inherited some of his sins. He was a real ball-breaker, and a man of many moods, which is understandable for a guy who faces death every time he goes to work.

There is no denying that he had plenty of charm when he wanted to turn it on. He had that all-American John Wayne macho image which so many fathers and sons find irresistible. A twenty-six-city flying tour adroitly guided by Shelly Saltman, who Evel called "my Jew press agent," generated tremendous interest in this absurd project.

I watched Knievel unravel a little bit each day as we approached the blast-off and in the final days he really started to come apart. He whacked out at an undersized NBC cameraman, he was surly at press conferences and he screamed foul abuses at our staff in public.

Each day got uglier than the last. I had a few words with him and quit drinking at his table, For the brighter moments there was the rugged beauty of the Canyon, the decent hospitality of the local townspeople and the wholesome attractiveness of one of my assistants, a nineteen-year-old kid named Margaux Hemingway.

Margaux is the granddaughter of Ernest Hemingway, and I was fascinated by her because the genetics couldn't have followed a closer pattern. She had the same blue eyes and the same broad face-bone structure of her grandfather.

She was tall, over five-foot-ten, and when she was animated she talked like she had marbles in her mouth, but this was part of her girlish charm. She was a stunner to look at and a perfect subject for the newsmen and photographers who wanted a change of pace from Knievel. She got a lot of coverage and I think you're going to be hearing more about this kid.

The final days here were hectic and the scene was madness. The bikers started to pour in a week before to take part in a series of races on the back lot. Then a battalion of Hell's

Angels rode in ominously. As the hour drew closer, the huge area that fenced off the spectators from the rim of the canyon looked like Cecil B. DeMille's *Sodom and Gomorrah* scene, but country style.

There were bloody brawls, naked broads, indiscriminate humping and enough drugs to keep Harlem happy for a week. The night before the jump they overturned a fully laden beer truck, ripped out the drinking fountains and set fire to the portable toilets.

David Frost, master of statistics and trivia, who was to be the anchorman on the closed-circuit broadcast, introduced himself to me the night before the blast-off. "I understand you're the press genius around here," he said. Then quickly, like he was testing me, he asked, "How many children does Knievel have?" I have a million other things on my mind and I answered right back, "Two boys."

"Aha, you forgot the daughter," he said coyly. I had just destroyed my own myth.

As the final countdown started, Knievel stood on a high platform and addressed the crowd in what might have been a farewell speech. A priest said the benediction and, with the cameras following him, Knievel slowly descended and walked slowly to the launch ramp. When he came alongside of us he bussed Mara on the cheek, then shook hands with me.

Close to my ear he said, "I know we had our differences, but it's been a rough week. I'm sorry." He was taut but solemn, a man resigned to his fate and seeking redemption. If ever I had pictured a guy going to the electric chair, this was it.

I don't know what really happened up there, and I don't

much care anymore, but Truax, the designer, said that because of metal stress the lever that opened the chute was triggered before Knievel was ready. But there were those who thought he hit the panic button.

Knievel may have been the star of this extravaganza, but his supporting cast of thousands made it for me. I never saw such a mix—cowboys, city slickers, dope peddlers, apple-cheeked country girls, groupies—and everyone seemed to be doing their own improvisations.

A few hours before the blast-off I took a quick walk through the edge of the crowd, skirting a pack of Hell's Angels. They looked as though they had been drawn by Al Capp. I asked one of them if he was a Knievel fan. A voice from the back of the pack said, "We ain't nobody's fans 'cept our own." A large walrus ambled over to me. "We just figure this asshole is gonna kill himself," he said, "and we don't want to miss it."

You had to be there.

Sincerely,

Harold

P.S. (*to the reader*): Goaded by the aggravation and harassment he suffered during his association with Knievel, Shelly Saltman wrote a book covering the canyon jump in detail, with special consideration for Evel's love trysts.

Shortly after the paperback was published, three men waited outside of Shelly's office in Los Angeles, Knievel and two muscular friends. Evel was carrying a baseball bat.

When Saltman came out of his office, the two shtarkers grabbed him while Evel whacked him across the arms, badly fracturing one of his wrists.

If Knievel had gone around whacking every writer who blew the whistle on him he could have broken Joe DiMaggio's record for hitting in consecutive games because there had been newspaper stories with pictures coast-to-coast about his extramarital curriculum. And able writers like Joe Eszterhas, Lucian Truscott and Bill Cardoso followed up with lengthy magazine articles and didn't leave much out.

Knievel's aggression was a despicable exercise and certainly not the act of a rational man. He was arrested and jailed. But if Knievel was motivated solely because Shelly's paperback was very close to being one of the worst-written, worst-edited books ever published, you might think about giving him a little time off for good behavior.

Howard Hughes, II

Dear Muffo:

Had lunch with Curley Harris the other day. Haven't seen Curley since Howard Hughes died. Curley, you know, worked for Howard in the early RKO days and later became one of his important New York contacts.

We've been trading Howard Hughes stories for years and today he comes up with one I never heard. Howard, you know, walks around in sneakers most of the time, not because he's a character, but because there's something wrong with the heel on his right foot.

Curley tells me he finds a little Italian shoemaker on upper Madison who makes a pair of shoes that corrects the heel problem and Howard loves the shoes.

Not long after that Howard almost gets himself killed when he crash-lands that plane in a Hollywood street. About six months after the crash, Curley gets a package in the mail. It's the shoes. Howard is wearing them when he cracks up. They're scorched and badly scuffed. A note in the package says, "Dear Curley: Please get these repaired." You'd think he'd say, "Get me a new pair made." No, he wants these repaired and there's hardly anything left of them.

"Do you think he's cheap?" I ask.

"Sometimes I wonder," says Curley. "He could argue with you over two dollars one minute and then he'd piss away five thousand chasing some silly broad."

I say, "Try this one on for size," and I tell him about the time I hang out at Walter Kane's apartment in Hollywood in the Fifties. It's also a hide-a-way for Hughes and I often run into him there.

One afternoon I'm sipping a martini and Howard is in the back bedroom on the phone. Kane comes running out. "Howard has to go someplace in a hurry and he wants to borrow your jacket," he says. We're both about the same size. Howard walks around in shirt sleeves or a sports shirt most of the time.

My jacket is a new cashmere job I just bought at Cy Devore's but am I going to refuse to loan my jacket to Howard Hughes? I take it off and give it to him. "Have it back to you tomorrow," he says.

I don't get it back tomorrow, or the next day or the next week. I keep bugging Kane and he keeps telling me Howard likes the jacket. One day Kane calls me. He says, "Howard just left here. He wants to keep the jacket, but he called Cy Devore and told him to give you another jacket."

I go over to Devore's. Cy meets me at the door. He tells me Hughes called and he takes me by the arm and leads me to the racks at the back of the store where he's got some stuff on sale.

Cy and I are close friends. Matter of fact, he is best man at my wedding. I say, "What the hell are you taking me back here with this crap for?" He's looking at me kind of strange. Finally he says, "Harold, I got to tell you the truth. When

Howard calls he says, 'Give him something on sale,' and that's the truth." I take the most expensive jacket in the store.

I don't think Hughes is cheap. It's just that rich guys get a bigger charge out of beating the price than poor guys even if it's just for a few bucks. They like to win, which is probably why they got all that dough in the first place.

The only rich guy I know who doesn't mind being taken is Muhammad Ali, who has given at least a million away to hustlers who come to him as friends-in-need. Ali once tells me, "There's a reason why God gave me the talent to make all this money. It's because through me he can help others who aren't so lucky. I feel better inside when I give my money away."

But Hughes has a thing about being pegged a sucker. Back when I'm living on the Coast, Howard is romancing a little movie actress who is a friend of Mara's. He gives her a Chevrolet as a gift. She has a date with him one night, but she's stuck on a job and she can't reach him by phone so she stands him up through no fault of her own. The next morning she goes out to get into her car, but it's gone. Hughes has it picked up.

While Curley and I are having coffee, Toots Shor, the boss of the joint, who has his own flair for throwing money around when he's got it, sits down with us. I'm just telling Curley the story of how Hughes tries to send me on a wild-goose chase to do the Jack Dempsey screen play just to get me out of town and Jack Kearns's name comes up.

"It's true that Kearns asked for a million for the rights to his character, crazy as it was, because he knew they couldn't do the picture without him," says Toots. "He wouldn't have taken nine-hundred-and-ninety-nine thousand, not even if he was starving. Here's the kind of guy he was.

"He comes in here a few years ago with some mark he's hustling and he's busted. I know how he likes to put on a big front grabbing the check so I figure instead of me picking it up I'll let him pay for it so I put a hundred-dollar bill in an envelope and have the maitre d' slip it to him.

"Kearns goes through the whole menu from the top down to champagne, brandy and cigars. When the check comes he signs it with a flourish and on the way out he tips the maitre d' my hundred-dollar bill. For a second I'm so mad I almost choke; then I sit down and laugh for five minutes."

Too bad Hughes didn't have that touch of class, but if he did have he wouldn't have wound up with that billion bucks, which isn't doing him any good now anyway.

Regards,

Harold

Muhammad Ali, II

NEW YORK
SEPTEMBER 29, 1976

Dear Muffo:

As you already know, Ali wins a squeaker over Ken Norton at the Yankee Stadium last night. He wins the fifteenth round and that's the round that decides the fight. Herbert Muhammad, Ali's manager, and Angelo Dundee both agree that if we don't stash the champ in my apartment the last week of training he never would have had the stamina to pull it off.

I don't know of any athlete who punishes his body as severely as Ali does and I'm afraid his lack of discipline will lop a few years off his active career. It's not that his training is so rigorous, noon and night. He never gets any rest.

Ali loves an audience and never brushes anybody whether its a mooch trying to put the bite on him or a couple of bus loads of screaming school kids who turn his training camp upside down. He's always tired and more than once I've seen him fall asleep during a press interview.

For this fight Ali trains three weeks in Showlow, Arizona, and three weeks at the Concord up in the Catskills. He's in pretty fair shape. By contract he has to train in New York City the week before the fight and the promoters have booked him and his entourage into the Essex House on Central Park South. I know this is going to be trouble.

Ali coming into New York is like a visitation from the Pope. They come from all over to pay homage. They also try to hustle him or give advice, the brothers and sisters from Harlem, the politicians, the hookers and the con men. He sees them all. He just stands around talking or doing his magic act. I've seen him go hoarse before a big fight, he'd talk to so many people. For serious champions like Joe Louis and Rocky Marciano it was work, rest, work, rest; and if a dame ever got into the camp all the alarms would go off.

The day we break camp at the Concord I tell Ali I think it would be a mistake to stay at the hotel.

"This last week is crucial," I tell him, "and you have to conserve your strength. You won't get a minute's rest at that hotel."

"You right," he says, "but I gotta stay someplace."

"How about my apartment," I say, "and we'll keep it a secret as long as we can?"

He's not too thrilled with being kept a secret but he realizes it is the logical move. "Let's do it," he says.

"On one condition," I tell him. "It's my house and it's up to me who can visit. That's your out."

"Okay," he says. "You the boss."

Mara takes Ali's suite at the Essex House and I move him into the master bedroom. We set up a videotape machine so he can study all the Norton fights, load the fridge with steaks, and everything is working out fine. I tell the press that he will be available at the gym every day and that's it. They're very cooperative.

Ali spends most of his time on the telephone or watching

the tube, but at least he's in bed resting. Madison Square Garden posts a security man on the door downstairs and Pat Patterson and Jim Brown, Ali's personal security guys, only show up to accompany him to the gym or to Central Park where he does his road work.

Of course, our secret is not a secret for very long. After the second day the whole West Side knows where he is staying. Patterson and Brown pick him up every morning at five-thirty and we go to the park where Ali does his roadwork on the bridle paths. If nobody is mugged between six and seven it's because all the muggers are jogging with Ali.

We have a few visitors like Gene Kilroy and Jerry Shabazz, close friends of Ali's, and Mailer come by with Norris. Dick Gregory stops by every day with a batch of health brews he has mixed. The neighbors are constantly ringing the bell and at Ali's insistence I let a few in each day for a quick chat. I can see that he is bored with this whole regimen, but he's relaxed and getting his rest.

The Thursday before the fight is the maid's day off and Mara comes in to straighten things out. Ali is sitting up in bed watching TV. He is wearing only his jogging pants. Mara does not know the Boxing Commission gives Ali a tricky plastic container for his urine analysis.

Mara spots this thing under the bed and picks it up in a sweeping move. But Ali forgets to close the lid and in a graceful arch, the contents come streaming out, all over him, the bed and the floor.

I know it is hard to picture Ali mortified with embarrassment, but I have never seen him so flustered. Mara, of course is speechless.

When I am talking to my mother that afternoon I tell her

what happened. You know my mother. If someone drops a fork, that means company is coming. If you step in dog shit, that means good luck. She says, "Beautiful, marvelous. You tell Ali I said that now he can't lose because that's the best kind of luck."

The night before the fight Ali's gorgeous wife, Veronica, her father, Horace, and a couple of Ali's kids stop by for a couple of hours, but they leave early. When Ali sees me getting dressed, he asks me where I'm going. I tell him I'm going to a party.

"You goin' off and leave me here alone?" he asks. I tell him not to worry, the security man will be on the door.

"But I'll be here all alone in the apartment," he says, whining like a kid.

"The fight's only twenty-four hours away," I tell him. "Try to get to sleep early. I'll be back in a few hours."

When I get back at midnight I look in on him and he's fast asleep. I am awakened several hours later by a rhythmic chant. It's Ali's voice and he keeps repeating, "Norton's got to go, Norton's got to go."

I look at the clock. It's four A.M. I peek into the other bedroom. Ali is sitting up in bed watching the tapes of his second Norton fight. He keeps waving his arms rhythmically as he repeats, "Norton's got to go." The fight is fifteen hours away and he's starting to psych himself up.

Ali is in full concentration the day of the fight and isn't saying much. I stay away from him. He has never had this opportunity before and he's making the most of it.

Later in the day I get a call from Budd Schulberg. He says I got to do him a favor. He's with Norman Lear and Ben Bradlee and they're dying to meet Ali. I tell him it's only hours before the fight and nobody's getting in to see Ali, but since it's my house there's no harm in his visiting me.

We are scheduled to leave for the stadium at six-thirty. They come up about five o'clock. The four of us sit down at the kitchen table over a bottle of Scotch. Ali stays in bed, spending a lot of time on the phone.

I go in and tell him Budd is visiting me with a couple of friends and I explain that Lear is the most important independent producer in television and that Bradlee is the most famous newspaper editor in the country. He never hears of either of them. But he likes Budd and he says to tell them he'll be out in a little while.

I'm watching Bradlee and Lear over the Scotch, Bradlee who can silence the whole *Washington Post* city room just by clearing his throat and Lear who forces the networks to juggle their prime time to meet his opposition. They're sitting there like two kids waiting for Santa Claus to come down the chimney. When I tell them Ali is coming out to see them, they're ecstatic.

"We don't want to bug him," Bradlee says. "We just want to say hello." When Ali finally comes out and sits down, they're speechless.

Pretty soon Gene Kilroy and the security men come up to get this show on the road. The whole block in front of my house is a mass of screaming fans. Ali's family is squashed in his waiting car. Mara and I get in Bradlee's limousine. It takes two police squad cars to clear the street. With a blast of sirens, we're off in the final stretch.

The fight won't go down in the annals as one of the great thrillers, but it was a close fight. Most of the score cards had it even going into the fifteenth. Ali came out dancing and won the round. You have to have a little something extra to rally after fourteen rounds and Ali had it that night. Some of the sports writers wrote that he was lucky, but they didn't know what my mother knew.

Sincerely,

Harold

Virginia Hill

NEW YORK
APRIL 20, 1977

Dear Muffo:

I'm just going over some pieces I do a long time ago and I run across a feature about a dame who is what B movies are all about. I'm interested because there's talk of one of the networks doing a mini-series on her, although there was a movie made of her life but they blew it and never really caught the character.

She dies of a heart attack about ten years ago in Switzerland and I guess her name don't mean much anymore, but when she hits New York in 1940 she's the answer to the gossip columnists' prayer. They get more mileage out of her than all the Humpty-Dumptys they're writing about.

To quote Spinoza, they must throw away the mold after they make her. Her name is Virginia Hill.

I'm doing the column at the time and she's a hot item. A press agent sends me a blurb about this tobacco heiress who's passing out money all over town like she's printing it and I write it. The day after it's in the paper I get a call. It's from this Virginia Hill. She's thanking me for writing about her and inviting me to a cocktail party in her suite at the Waldorf-Astoria.

I go to the party and she's got one of the biggest suites in the Waldorf. When I meet her I see I've been taken. She don't talk like any tobacco heiress, more like "chitlins and hog heads," but she's a pretty girl, good figure and a great personality. She's got Xavier Cugat playing the music and she's apologizing because it's only half his orchestra. Couldn't fit all his eighteen pieces into the joint.

Virginia's on the town every night with dinner parties of fifteen and twenty. She hardly knows any of the people she's hosting and she's handing out fifty-dollar tips to maitre d's, which is a pretty good touch in them days. She pays all the tabs with cash.

Everybody's wondering how even a tobacco heiress has all that cash to spread around. She tells the insiders that she owns a piece of the biggest horse book in Chicago, but some of them know this is not exactly true. A guy named Joe Epstein, who runs the biggest book in Chicago, is completely nuts about her and she owns all of Joe Epstein, which is probably better. He gives her anything she wants and all she wants is cash.

It is plain that she is not true blue to Joe Epstein because Virginia's got all kinds of action going for her. For a while she is having a thing with Miguelito Valdez, the Cuban singer and bongo player who is a current rage. Then she meets Joe Adonis, and it's a romance right off. They go to the La Conga nightclub one evening and Valdez is hanging around. Adonis tells Valdez to get lost and in passing mentions it wouldn't be easy for a bongo player to play the bongos with two broken arms.

This romance lasts for a while then there's an interesting switch. Virginia becomes enamored with Benny Siegel. Bugsy starts guilding a hotel and gambling casino in a place called Las Vegas and he keeps tapping The Mob for huge sums of money. They have their doubts about building a place in some barren desert town.

I am curious about the switch from Adonis to Siegel. I think that these guys got a code about touching each other's women. Maybe I get this out of a gangster movie. Anyway, when I'm in Florida in '46 I ask Adonis whatever happened with him and Virginia. Adonis, who has strong Sicilian macho bloodlines, says, "Great broad, but she was out in front all the time, giving orders and fighting me for the dinner checks. That can de-ball you when you got a broad always grabbing the checks. So I hedged her off to Benny."

Virginia and Bugsy sneak off to Mexico that year and get married, but things aren't going too well for him with his Las Vegas project. It's just after the war and it's hard getting building materials. Everything costs triple and The Mob's beefing about the dough they're shelling out. The hotel is only half built, but the casino is finished and Siegel opens the joint. It's called The Flamingo. It's a bust and now The Syndicate is up in arms. The board of directors meet and vote to have Siegel rubbed out, but his close friend Meyer Lansky pleads for another chance for him. Lansky blames all the trouble on Virginia Hill. "That broad is running his life," says Meyer, "and his balls were always bigger than his brains."

Some time later they reopen The Flamingo and it does well. Some of the more far-sighted members of the board see Las Vegas as a very promising place, but Siegel has let it drop that Las Vegas is his personal territory. This word does not set well at all with The Boys. Again they vote to erase him and this time Lansky can't save him.

Around this time Virginia gets a load of cash from Joe

Epstein and flies off to Paris. It is rumored that she got the message. A few days later Siegel is in their home in Beverly Hills. He is with another guy and by design Bugsy is seated on a couch facing the window. Someone sticks a carbine through the window and shoots his eyes out.

The tumult dies down after a while and we don't hear much of Virginia until 1950. Remember Estes Kefauver, the tall, lanky guy who used to wear the coonskin cap, who ran for vice-president on the ticket with Adlai Stevenson? Well, nobody would have heard of him if he hadn't been the chairman of the Senate Crime Investigative Committee. They had it live on television in the early days and the camera kept focusing on Frank Costello's hands. Most of gangland's top names paraded before that committee but the prettiest witness was Virginia Hill.

The committee would meet in the morning with the witnesses and sift through a lot of the questions because there were some things they didn't want to ask on live TV. Ernie Mittler, a former assistant D.A. who became a top aide to Kefauver, is a friend of mine and I manage to get some of the choice morsels.

Virginia is not a very cooperative witness and one morning when they're behind closed doors, Senator Tobey is trying to establish where she is getting all that cash. Tobey, a cherubic little guy from New Hampshire has always got a Bible with him and he keeps quoting from the psalms. He's about as well equipped to be investigating gangsters as Shirley Temple, but you know politics.

He keeps asking Virginia who she got all that cash from and she keeps saying she got it from her boy friend. "But why would he give you all that money?" Tobey keeps repeating. Virginia gets pissed off. "You really want to know why?" she finally answers.

"Yes," Tobey says. "I want to know why."

"Then I'll tell you why. Because I'm the best cocksucker in town."

Needless to say, Tobey all but swallowed his Bible.

They don't make them like that anymore, do they, Muffo.

Regards,

Harold

Hunter Thompson

NEW YORK
JUNE 7, 1978

Dear Muffo:

Just got your note about the Hunter Thompson piece in *Rolling Stone*. I go way back with Thompson when he was writing sports in some jerk-water town. He's a good guy and a hell of a talent, but a little weird. When he told me he was stuck with his *Rolling Stone* piece and needed an interview with Muhammad to make it, I told him Ali was coming into New York. I suggested he book a seat on the same plane with him from Chicago and I gave him the flight number. I also told Ali that Thompson would be on the flight.

When I read his piece in *Rolling Stone* I thought he left out one of the best parts so I write a letter to the magazine and here's a copy of it:

"After reading Dr. Hunter S. Thompson's prodigious piece (Last Tango in Vegas) it certainly would appear that nothing was left out. But not quite. I thought the most frantic scene of the wild evening occurred in the staid lobby of the Park Lane Hotel just before the doctor got to see Ali.

"After Muhammad brushed Thompson on the plane trip from Chicago to New York, the doctor arrived at the Plaza Hotel, where I originally booked him, as I did Ali. But Ali

239

changed his mind the last minute and checked into the Park Lane about five hundred yards up the street.

"I try to explain this to Thompson, but he isn't buying it. He is convinced he is the victim of some dastardly CIA plot. Blue smoke is coming out of his nostrils, scented with Wild Turkey, and paranoia has set in. Finally he simmers down a bit and I tell him my chauffeur will pick him up and take him to the Park Lane. Meantime I will run over there and square things with Ali. 'Meet me in the lobby of the Park Lane,' I tell him. 'Be sure and wait there until I come down.'

"I go up to Ali's suite wondering how I'm going to explain Dr. Thompson. No way. Ali is already in bed. I say, 'Ali, the guy you brushed on the plane is downstairs. You were supposed to meet up with him and he came all the way from Colorado to interview you.'

"Ali don't know Hunter Thompson from Kafka. He thinks for a second. 'You mean that crazy hippie on the plane who was trying to talk to me?' he asks. 'I just thought he wanted my autograph. Okay, bring him but right away 'cause I got to get to sleep.'

"I dash down to the lobby to pick up Thompson, but he's not there. The Park Lane is only two minutes from the Plaza. I left him ten minutes ago. My chauffeur is with him so he can't get lost. Where the hell is he? I can see Ali turning off the lights, and that's the end of the interview. And in Thompson's state he'll be convinced that Ali is not in the hotel or that there is no Muhammad Ali.

"He walks in five minutes later followed by the chauffeur with his luggage. I tell him Ali is waiting. He insists on checking in first.

"Now he is at the desk, reaching into his jacket for his

credit card. Suddenly he is frantically going through all his pockets.

"'Holy shit, my wallet! Who the fuck took my wallet? It's a goddamned plot,' he snarls through clenched teeth, shattering his cigarette holder. His eyes roll and his arms flail. I think he is going catatonic. Dr. Thompson looks like he is on a worse bummer than Dr. Jekyll.

"He screams for a bellboy to bring his luggage over, and he dumps it in the center of the lobby. One piece looks like a bed-roll. Another is a large, strange-looking satchel. The last time I see this type of gear is on the heads of two Sherpa guides thirty miles north of Katmandu. There is also a tape recorder, an attaché case and a large brown paper bag, and it's all spread out on this beautiful marble floor, right in the center of traffic.

"Thompson attacks the attaché case and turns it upside down. No wallet. Now he attacks the satchel and his hands keep flipping things up in the air like a juggler tossing Indian clubs. First a bottle of Heineken. It caroms gently off the bag and rolls across the lobby. Then a bottle of Wild Turkey, a shoe and another bottle of Heineken. The assistant manager is aiming dirty looks at me from his post at the desk. I shrug back like I don't know the nut on the floor.

"I look down at Thompson groveling on all fours in his sneakers and two-dollar baseball cap and say to myself, if I take this kook up to the suite, Muhammad will probably put the wrath of Allah on my head. If I don't take him up, Thompson will probably mace me all over the Sheep Meadow in Central Park across the street. A notion crosses my mind. Where do you get a snub-nosed .38 at this hour?

"By now the doctor reaches the bowels of the satchel and

comes up with a shaving kit. He opens it. Eureka! There is the wallet. He had put it in his shaving kit. Doesn't everybody?

"At last he checks in and with much trepidation I take him up to Muhammad's suite.

"I don't know how the doctor did it but he came through. The interview with Muhammad was one of the best I've seen and I thought the overall 'Last Tango in Vegas' was brilliant even though he did call me a pig fucker."

Regards,

Harold

Damon Runyon

Dear Muffo:

I'm walking down Sullivan Street in the Village yesterday when I see a commotion. There's a bearded guy stretched out on the pavement and a couple of fellows have a strangle hold on a wild-eyed guy who is yelling, "You fox-in-the-bush bastard, I'll kill you." When the tumult dies down I find out that the wild-eyed one punched the other guy out simply because he doesn't like beards.

Now I begin to wonder, what can a guy have against beards? In the great protest meetings in the late Sixties any guy with long hair is the prime target for a cop's billy. Cops, hard-hats and even the Establishment views it as a badge of defiance and they're positive that anybody with locks below the collar line is either a Communist, a draft dodger or gay. Now you see cops and hard-hats and even baseball players wearing their hair long. I figure the antihirsute syndrome has gone the route of hula-hoops. But now a guy gets flattened for wearing a beard.

As I walk uptown I start clocking the beards. I'm amazed there's so many and I figure, not to worry, that what I saw was an isolated case. I note that the smaller the guy, the bigger the beard. I also note that some guys look great in beards and some guys look comical and I think about a column Damon Runyon once did that offers an interesting analogy.

One day Runyon asks me why I seldom wear a hat and I tell him. I don't know he's going to do a column about hats. Let me give you an excerpt from it:

"I have often wondered why residents of New York City become no-hatters and I spent all of Tuesday's hot afternoon carrying on a poll of the question, 'Why do you go without a hat?' and only one person gave me an answer I deem fairly sound. He was Harold Conrad, a tall, angular newspaper pal of mine who wears a hat in the winter but goes hatless in the summer.

"'Because,' said Harold, 'I do not look good in a hat.'

"I studied hatless Harold's physiognomy at length, noting the style of his head and the shape of his ears and other points and then I conjured to mind a picture of him in a hat and I said to myself, Runyon, the guy has something there.

"Of course not every man can hope to be a Runyon in a hat but every man can conceal from public view certain indiscretions of nature when she was making their heads."

The last few lines give me the clue as to why some guys grow beards although they don't always work out as a plus, but Runyon was so right about hats.

Did it ever occur to you why guys like Bing Crosby, Fred Astaire and Gene Kelly wear hats most of the time when they're not in front of the camera and often when they are? It's because the hat covers the toupee, and I find that no matter how suave or nonchalant a guy who wears a toupee is he's always sensitive about it. Is it on straight? Does it look too phony? Howard Cosell is one of the few guys not uptight about his piece. When I first see him around the fight scene he wears a rug that looks like an abandoned robin's nest. Now he sports a wall-to-wall job, Rolls-Royce style.

I get nostalgic about Runyon, going back and reading that old column. It is printed in 1945, the year before he dies. It is a shame he is not on the scene today and it's a greater shame the last generations know so little about him.

He was a super-star best-seller in his time, and twenty-six movies were made from his works, some of which he produced himself. There were big winners like *Guys and Dolls, Little Miss Marker, The Lemon Drop Kid, A Slight Case of Murder, Lady for a Day* and *Pocket Full of Miracles,* among others.

The late Joe Meyers, then publisher of Avon Books, who printed most of Runyon's soft cover stuff, tells me about six years after Runyon dies that he can't move Damon's stuff. "Whenever you hear Runyon's name mentioned, it's the Damon Runyon Cancer Fund," says Meyers. "People forget what a great stylist he was and all they think of is cancer."

There's been a couple of books written about Runyon but I think they miss the mark. He was not an easy guy to sketch, especially if you didn't know him.

Runyon was an ex-alcoholic who didn't get into the big money until he put the bottle aside. Once he made it he flaunted it. He had an island home in Miami Beach, a place in New York and a place in Beverly Hills. He had race horses and fancy jewelry, but I don't think he was a happy man. He had two kids from an early marriage and he wasn't too happy about them.

He had a flashy ex-showgirl wife and he gave her anything she wanted. He was nuts about her, but there was a problem. She had a penchant for young guys and all of Broadway knew it, but he played it straight like nothing was happening, which was a sad thing for a man with his dignity.

Cancer struck in the early 1940s and after I get out of the army I spend a lot of time with him. He likes my writing style and lets me do the radio version of his Joe and Ethel Terp characters, but it don't work out because his stuff is not just for the ear.

He overcame a loss of speech and would write terse gems on a little pad during conversation. I think somehow his perceptions heightened after he lost his speech. He was writing better than ever.

He was writing twelve short stories a year for *Collier's* and maintained his column as one of Hearst's top stars. He wrote one short story that tickled the insiders who knew about his problem with his wife. It was about an affluent New York bookmaker who had a runner who was completely devoted to him. The bookie has a bad streak and goes broke. The bookie's wife duns him for an expensive mink coat and he buys it for her with his last dough. Then she leaves him and he dies of a broken heart, without a penny. They have to bury him in Potters Field.

After he dies the wife screams that somebody stole her mink coat and there's no trace of it. Where's the coat? The punch is it's covering his grave in potter's field. The little runner stole the mink and covered the grave with it to keep him warm. I'm sure Runyon was trying to tell his wife something.

Runyon kept going through a series of operations. The cancer was spreading. After one operation I'm sitting in his room at the Memorial Hospital when a bulletin comes over the radio that President Roosevelt has just died. He scribbles a note to call his office that he will cover the funeral.

I say, "How the hell can you get out of bed to go to Washington? You just had an operation." But he insists. Hearst had been murdering F.D.R. in print for years and I wondered how he was going to handle this. He wrote a column about a guy who is standing with his kid, watching the funeral cortege go by. The kid says to his father, "Daddy, if he was such a bad man like you say, how come all these people are crying for him?" Then he went on to write a glowing piece about F.D.R.'s accomplishments. The father was unmistakably Hearst and I often wonder what the old publisher thought when he read that one.

Runyon was a lonely, unhappy man in those last years, but still very much in love with his wife. Before the Christmas holidays in '45 he scribbles a note asking me to call her in Florida and find out when she is coming to New York. I call her and she says she isn't coming. I plead with her and she says, "You keep him company, he'll be all right."

I don't know how to tell this to him, so I keep quiet. He takes a big sheet of paper and in large letters prints: "Goddamn it, when is she coming?" I break him up for a minute when I answer, "Damon, you don't have to yell at me." Finally I tell him. His eyes well up and he turns away.

One day I really think I have it made. I'm sitting in the apartment with him when the phone rings. It's Darryl Zanuck, boss of 20th Century-Fox, where Damon had most of his successes. Zanuck says, "Tell Damon I have the perfect property for him. I want him to come out to Hollywood to write and produce. He can name his own ticket."

I relay the message to Runyon and he scribbles, "Marvelous, tell him I'll get back to him in a few days." Then he gives me a sly look and scribbles another note. It reads: "Start shopping for some fancy luggage. You're going with me as associate producer." I could have kissed him.

The next day he goes to his doctor and tells him about the trip to L.A. The doctor says there is no way he can leave New York because the Memorial Hospital is one of the few places in the country which has cobalt treatment which is vital to him. They don't have it on the coast yet, so that's that.

Runyon died about eight months later. I miss him but I know he's still around. They sowed his ashes over Broadway from an airplane and you know I live just off Broadway.

I hate to end this on such a somber note, so I got to tell you my favorite Runyon story and you won't find it in any of his biographies.

Four of us are sitting at the Round Table in the Cub Room of the Stork Club one night, Runyon, myself, Walter Winchell and Sherman Billingsley, who owns the joint. Runyon is torching for his wife, Winchell's girl has run off with Frank Gallop, the announcer, Billingsley's girl is shacking up with a dance director, and I've broken up with my girl.

As us four contenders for cuckoldry seek solace in union,

Runyon raises his hand in a gesture that says, "Hold every-thing, fellows," then he quickly scribbles a note and tosses it out to the center of the table. Winchell picks it up and reads it aloud.

He reads: "Stop worrying, guys. Nobody ever ruined a good cunt by screwing it."

Sincerely,

Harold

Comic Strips, II

NEW YORK
NOVEMBER 6, 1979

Dear Muffo:

Sad to report, our friend Al Capp has just joined Ham
Fisher some place up there in Cartoonland. My mother put
me on the spot. She used to say, "Don't talk bad about the
dead." She also used to say, "Always tell the truth." Since I
have a choice, I've got to tell you that Fisher was a cheap,
petty transparent bullshit artist. When his wife showed the
good sense to leave him he would corner anybody, even
bellboys in the hotel lobby, and tell them what an ingrate
she was, and worse.

His feud with Capp accelerated down through the years.
There were phone calls and screaming in the middle of the
night. He spread scurrilous lies about Capp's daughter when
she was in college, one being that she was pregnant. Al
didn't take all this lying down. One day while reading the
"Li'l Abner" strip I thought I saw a pig that looked familiar.
Now it isn't often that you see pigs you know. I took another
look and realized that Capp had given the pig a caricature of
Fisher's face. The pig became a steady feature and it drove
Fisher crazy, but if he wanted to be called Ham, that was his
problem.

251

I first met Capp when "Li'l Abner" was just starting to catch on. He was sharp, witty and a serious supporter of liberal causes. He was also a marvelous story-teller and his subject was usually sex. I wondered at his unusual sex drive, which led him to extremes and finally proved his undoing. He would always tell me in detail about his conquests and they were often movie stars or the wives of prominent men.

He would give me phone numbers of girls he had taken out and plead with me to make dates with them with the stipulation that I had to give him a rundown on what happened and also report what they said about him. Al, you know, was only a kid when he lost a leg high up on the hip in an auto accident. You remember how he moved around slowly with a painful-looking limp. My amateur Freudian diagnosis of his sex mania was that he had to keep proving to himself that he was a whole man.

At his insistence, I called one little actress who lived around the corner from me at the Rehearsal Club. Frankly, I didn't have much resistance in these matters. She was pretty and bright and a serious actress. We had a few drinks and some intelligent conversation and I had to get her home by eleven because she had an audition in the morning.

At two A.M. my phone rings. "Okay, okay, give me the rundown." It's Capp and he's breathless. I laid a story on him that would have topped any of the scenes in *Deep Throat*.

"And what did she say about me?" he asked.

"Al," I said, "she told me you had the biggest cock in town and that you were the greatest."

"You betcha, you betcha," he said. "And she knew how to handle it. What a performer."

Now Capp had to know that I knew she never said that, but it didn't seem to matter. What the girl really said was, "I was disappointed in Al. He's so bright and talented, but all he did was talk dirty and try to get me into the bedroom. I know this sounds awful but all I had was a mental picture of him taking off his wooden leg and it turned me off. Maybe if I had been in love it would have been different." That's when I began to understand Capp's problem and realized that most of the stories about his conquests were probably not true.

He had one great gimmick that must have paid off because there was a prize at stake. A couple of years before the *Li'l Abner* movie was made, Capp would go into a town and hold an audition for the Daisy Mae role and of course at least fifty young dames would show up and he would list the choice ones and their phone numbers in his little black book. I know it worked because I inherited a Daisy Mae contestant when he held an audition at the Beverly Hills Hotel.

Al was very successful on the lecture circuit and he liked to book universities because, as he once told me, "That's where all the young pussy is concentrated." He was also a welcome guest on the network talk shows and was an amusing panelist. But suddenly he made a 180-degree turn and I have no idea what the catalyst was. It must have been something drastic.

In the sixties, when the kids were making their most provocative stand in the history of American youth, Al took after them in an endless, vituperative campaign. He lashed out at their morals, their long hair and their stand on the Vietnam War. He had become a hawk and his politics moved to the right of the right. He became such a bore on the talk shows that they stopped booking him. But Al's new posture didn't mean that he had switched to old ladies. He was still chasing the young chippies. He was like a guy with the Bible in one hand and a vibrator in the other.

Then the roof caved in on him when he was on a speaking engagement in a small Midwestern city. The details were never very clear, but he got caught putting the arm on a couple of local girls and the city fathers rode him out of town. The story broke in the newspapers and he was disgraced. He completely dropped out of public life till his obit showed up yesterday.

I've got a tip for the angels. Don't believe anything Ham Fisher says. And if you're around Al Capp, and you're a lady angel, don't bend over.

Sincerely,

Harold

Lansky

Dear Muffo:

Down here in our old stamping grounds with Mara for a few weeks. She's getting some back treatment from Dr. Mike and after all these years I think she's finally getting straightened out. She's even talking about going back to ballet class next month. Remember she had to quit the business right after she played Marilyn Monroe's girl friend in a bit of a turkey called *Let's Make Love*.

As you know, I've been in a lot of towns and there are stories for every one of them, but this is one burg I can get sentimental about. It was here that I first hooked up with a loud-mouth, fresh kid named Cassius Clay and we had a hell of a run together, from Zaire to Dublin, form Malaysia to Manila. He's retired now, but now he's talking about fighting again. I told him he ought to forget it.

I think I get a little touch of the haunts here last night after the sun goes down. The ghosts are all over the place, apparitions like Winchell, Raft, Joe E. Lewis and the gangsters.

Although most of them are gone now, those mob guys never seem to fade away. They keep popping up in movies and television shows, and whenever I see them I get a kick out of the fact that I watched them from a ringside seat when they were still the lords of the underworld.

Many years ago, right after I finish up at the Colonial Inn, Westbrook Pegler asks me if it didn't bother my conscience working for "those dirty bastards." I tell him no. The morality did cross my mind, but only briefly. There were more than a hundred other straight people doing their regular jobs at the Colonial.

I'd be lying if I said I wasn't fascinated by The Mob and I've seen important politicians and big society names go dry-mouthed when they talked to them. I think I figure out the chemistry. The gangsters have an aura of menace around them that titillates those souls whose biggest thrill is breaking par or goosing their secretaries. It's like petting lions and tigers who are housebroken.

To me, Benny Siegel is always the star and his friendship for George Raft intrigues me. George, who was one of the biggest earners in Hollywood at the time, came up with some important money to try and bail Siegel out when he was in trouble.

During the ugly Un-American Activities Committee mess, several years after Benny was killed, Humphrey Bogart went around collecting money for a fund to help the accused writers and actors who were going to Washington to defend themselves. Although Bogart and Raft aren't close friends, they made several pictures together, so Bogart goes over to George's house to put the bite on him in the name of the "Unholy Ten." Now Raft is one of those guys who never reads anything in his life except movie scripts and the sports section of his newspaper.

Bogart explains the situation to him and George, usually a

likable reasonable fellow, says, "Yeah, now you come to me. Where the hell were all you guys when Benny Siegel was in trouble?" Bogart knew he couldn't top that one and left without a donation.

Last night I think I am touched by déjà vu because I see Meyer Lansky in the flesh, the lone survivor of my four bosses from the Colonial Inn. Lansky has had great billing over the years: like, "The Mob runs America and Lansky runs the Mob" and "Lansky is the mystery man behind organized crime in America today."

Last night I go to the opening of a musical in Miami Beach and after the show on the way out I spot Lansky, the man who inherited the whole pie for a while. He is standing by his seat with his bodyguard, waiting for the crowd to leave. He hasn't changed much. That perpetual smile has never left him, but the crinkles around his eyes are now deep furrows. I can't resist going over to him.

It's thirty-three years since we see each other and naturally he doesn't recognize me offhand. I mention the Colonial Inn and the smile dissolves into a thinking frown. There's a long pause, then he says in a soft voice, "Harold! Sure I remember. How you doing, kid?" and the smile is back in focus. There's another long pause and he nods his head slowly. "Sure, I remember. Those were the days."

Regards,

Harold

Superman

Dear Muffo:

I used to be a regular movie-goer until I start getting bored with the endless parade of smart-assed robots and exotic mechanical toys that flit across the screen, ingenious as they are. They just don't turn out many adult movies anymore.

Last night I make an exception and go to see *Superman II.* They tell me that *Superman I* has already grossed over two hundred million, that *Superman II* will top that and that *Superman III* is already on the drawing board.

That is not why I go. Bestsellers never impress me. I go because Superman was a dear friend of mine. I'm talking about George Reeves, the original Superman who created the role for television (no relation to the actor Christopher Reeve who is doing the movie). I want to see what they are doing with the character.

I first meet George Reeves in the Air Force, during the war. He has just finished starring in a picture with Claudette Colbert called *So Proudly We Hail,* and he gets rave notices. The critics are predicting a brilliant Hollywood future for him.

A week after the picture is released, George winds up in the Service. When he finally gets out, so do Tyrone Power,

Clark Gable, Jimmy Stewart, Bob Montgomery and a long list of others. George gets lost in the shuffle and has to take roles in a lot of bad B pictures to keep eating.

Television, still new, is groping for ideas and someone gets the notion to do a series with Superman, based on the character in the comic strip created by Schuster and Seigal. They cast George and it is he who brings the unlikely character to life, with all the nuances. He also writes and directs several of the shows.

Although the series starts before my son Casey is born, he grows up on Superman. They must shoot at least a couple of hundred shows and he has seen most of them twice like millions and millions of other kids around the world, English kids, Japanese kids, French kids, dubbed in their own languages.

Off the screen, George is pretty close to Clark Kent, a bumbling, naive, decent sort of guy with a good sense of humor. He is also a solid, natural actor. He sings well and accompanies himself creditably on the guitar.

It's 1959 and I'm in Miami Beach. I just sell an option on *No. 1*, that play you liked and am doing a final polish. Mara is doing an act at the new Americana Hotel which just opens in Bal Harbour.

One night we stop off for a drink at a little bar and who is sitting a few tables from us: "Faster than a speeding bullet, more powerful than a locomotive, able to leap over tall buildings in a single bound. . . . It's Superman!"

He is with Lenore Lemmon, a girl we knew for years and they don't have to tell us this is a hot romance. It's obvious. Lenore has been a meteor in the galaxy of the idle rich, dubbed Café Society, now called the Jet Set. How she remained in this orbit is always a mystery because she never had more than a little front money.

They join our table and after a bit George asks me to go up to the bar and have a drink with him. Then he tells me his sad story. He's flat on his ass and doesn't even have enough of his own money to get out of town.

I find this hard to believe. I assume he's living off the dividends of his enormously successful show. He tells me they paid him off in peanuts and promises every week and when they finished shooting the series his relation with Superman ended. There are no residual deals.

I say, "George, someone must have laid some kryptonite on you." He laughs. We used to have a running gag on kryptonite. As any fool knows, kryptonite is a substance which can diminish Superman's powers and eventually destroy him.

But kryptonite is no laughing matter. From the beginning the Hollywood laboratories have been developing it in many forms. It manifests itself in the small print of contracts, in the double talk of agents and in the awesome power that radiates from the powerful studios. For a long time artists and creators had no immunity against it until the guilds discover some antidotes.

As I look at Superman on the bar stool next to me, haggard and depressed, I suggest I write an act for him since the whole world knows his face and since he sings and plays the guitar well enough. But he is spiritless and insecure. He says no.

We hang out together on the beach for a few days, then he and Lem take off. Almost a year passes and I don't hear a word from Superman. As I am reading The Times one morning and jump from page one to the obit page in my morning ritual, I am stunned by a shocker. Superman has been destroyed.

George Reeves leaves a party of revelers in the living room, goes up to the bedroom and blows his brains out. But it is not really the bullet that destroys him, it is the kryptonite.

Maybe Superman still lives for some people, but not for me.

Sincerely,

Harold

The Brooklyn Dodgers and Thomas Wolfe

NEW YORK
OCTOBER 27, 1981

Dear Muffo:

I'm driving through Brooklyn the other day for the first time in many years and I make it a point to detour over to Bedford Avenue to pay homage to the shrine of my youth—Ebbets Field—home of the Brooklyn Dodgers, who have been missing for a couple of decades.

It must be more than coincidence that I am listening to the third game of the Los Angeles Dodgers–New York Yankees World Series on the car radio as I drive past the hallowed ground. Sitting high on the outfield where Babe Herman used to get hit on the noggin with fly balls is a huge apartment building.

The Dead Sea Scrolls left over from the first century B.C. revealed the secrets of a whole civilization. The crumbling Colosseum in Rome where the Christians were the blue-plate special for the lions still stands to give you a glimpse of what once was the stage for the Roman Empire. But here on this sacred site, not one artifact. Not even a fungo bat lying around or a couple of spike marks to show evidence of the lost Brooklyn Dodger civilization.

When you talk to an old Brooklyn fan, you get the impression that in the Fifties a space ship swooped down, picked up their whole Dodger team and took them to another planet, where they were recycled. They are now robots who established a base in Los Angeles and infiltrated the National League, claiming the name of Dodgers.

When I was on the *Brooklyn Eagle,* the Dodgers were the big story of the day no matter what else was going on in the world. The final edition didn't go to press until the ballgame was over and the paper was on the street less than fifteen minutes after the final out, with a complete box score.

There was pain and trauma in the streets of Brooklyn when the Dodgers lost, which seemed like most of the time. The bitching and post mortems went on in the bars until closing time. A principal forum at one o'clock in the morning was Bickford's Restaurant on the edge of Boro Hall, which was Dodger heartland.

Bickford's was the hangout for sportswriters, linotypers, touts, bookmakers, hookers and Brooklyn Heights insomniacs. There was a big news stand out in front and many of the customers would dawdle over coffee waiting for the first edition of *The New York Times* to come out, which was usually around one-twenty A.M. The *Times* had the charts and prices of the West Coast race tracks for the bookmakers and the box score of all the games for the baseball nuts.

I'm sitting over coffee this night, and it is the eve of a four-game series between the Dodgers and the Giants. To a Brooklyn Dodger fan the Giants are the Redcoats, the Hessians, the Confederates and the Huns all rolled up in one. The hatred is unadulterated and tomorrow's opener is the topic of the night. It is not unusual for a guy to be arguing with another guy four tables away and it doesn't take long for two other guys at remote tables to join the conversation.

While I'm listening to one guy yelling, "We gotta pitch Mungo tomorrow," a guy stakes a seat at my table and puts his coffee mug down. He's a whale of a man with wild eyes and recalcitrant hair. He looks like "somebody," but I can't place him.

The big fellow sits silently over his coffee, his head cocked to catch all the streams of dialogue. Every once in a while he lets out a loud snort, which I interpret as derision. Could he be a Giant fan in this Dodger sanctuary? Finally, he says to me in a Dixie drawl, "There's not one bum on that Dodger team who could carry Bill Terry's bat." Terry is a .400 hitter who leads the Giants.

I have to agree with him even though such a remark in Bickford's is heresy. After he gets up to leave, I am curious and I collar Hymie "Bankroll," an erudite bookmaker who seems to know everything. I ask Hymie if he knows the big guy who was sitting at my table. "You a writer for Christ sake and you don't know who he is? That's Thomas Wolfe. Wrote a big winner called *Look Homeward Angel.* I read it. Heavy stuff."

Of course I know who Thomas Wolfe is although I had never read him. I am more shocked than surprised. Thomas Wolfe here in Bickford's and talking baseball? It didn't match up.

I run into Wolfe on the average of twice a week the next couple of months. The second time I meet him I leave the restaurant when he does. "You walking?" I ask. "Yes," he says. I say, "I am going this way." He says, "Then I'm going that way."

It was his not too subtle manner of letting me know our

relationship was confined to Bickford's and that to him walking in the night was a solo venture reserved for wrestling with problems of the mind.

One night, out of nowhere he says, "I've been wanting to tell this to a sportswriter for a long time. If I want to read literature I'll go to Shakespeare, or Tolstoy or Conrad. Not you, your Uncle Joseph," he adds, making a joke and smiling only with his eyes. "But when I read the sports pages I want to read how, why, and what's the score. I don't want to have to suffer through 'The crimson sun sank slowly beyond the stark steel girders' or find out that 'the dew glistens on the aquamarine grass.'"

I get his point. Up to then I used to think that was good writing. I ask him if he is working on a book and he says "Yes," he has been for some time. "No," he is not sure of the title yet. "Yes," he does live in Brooklyn Heights.

One evening when I am working on the night desk, a story comes in on a homicide in south Brooklyn. A mail truck driver who picks up the cash at the postal substations and is always armed stops by his bar on the way home and knocks over a half-dozen beers.

The Dodgers have lost another close one that afternoon and the bistro is seething with "shoulda—woulda—couldas." One guy is ranting about Dolph Camilli, whose error cost the Dodgers the game. The mailman gets into the argument and one word leads to another. When the guy says, "I've had it up to here with them bums. They ought to be thrown out of the league," the mailman pulls the pistol from his holster and shoots him between the eyes. He is charged with first-degree murder.

I run into Wolfe at Bickford's that night and I recount the

story for him. He listens intently and a full minute passes before he answers. "Poetic justice," he says.

That's the last time I saw Thomas Wolfe. His book comes out about ten months later. He called it *Of Time and the River.*

Warmest,

Harold

Dear Muffo:

If the significance of the above date has eluded you, let me remind you, my friend, that it is just a few months shy of forty years that our correspondence started. It took me back to the last night we spent together before you first went away.

You and I were sitting on a bench bordering the Miami Bay front with Smilin' Jack Singer, the promising young Hearst writer. I recall the night vividly. The full moon looked like it had been put up there by one of those Florida press agents. Over the rustle of the palms we could hear the wail of a saxophone in the band of the Royal Palm Casino behind us. We were waiting to pick up our dates, three gorgeous kids in the line. Wonder what they look like now.

Was it Jack Singer or you who said you felt guilty indulging in this tranquility while our friends in London were spending the night in bomb shelters. We all knew guys who had already enlisted. It was Singer and not you who said, "Let's not talk about that tonight. This might be our last fling."

You went off to Europe to cover the mess there, Singer

went off to the Pacific as a war correspondent, and I went home and wrote a flag-waving column. It must have been a pretty good piece because after I read it in the paper the next day, I went out and enlisted in the Air Force.

If you're wondering where the Montovani background music is, Muffo, indulge me for a few graphs. This is one of those nights when the past is jumping up at me.

Singer joined a task force in the Pacific and was assigned to the carrier *Wasp*, remember? I never told you I received a V-mail letter from him some six weeks after he sent it. He was very up, telling me about his ambitions, but to me it was the saddest letter I ever read, because a few days before I received it, I had already heard the news. He was writing in the ward room where the *Wasp* took a direct hit from a torpedo that sent it to the bottom.

Muffo, I just decided maybe memory lane is not my bag. I checked Funk and Wagnall's for a definition of nostalgia, and it said: "A desire to return, in thought and fact, to a former time in one's life." I don't want to go back, Muffo. I want to know where the action is going to be tomorrow.

Sincerely,

Harold

Index